Living Dangerously

Stories of Men Who Risk Death Daily — On the Job

Edited by John Barnett

DOW JONES BOOKS
PRINCETON, NEW JERSEY

Introduction

The thirst for adventure runs deep in the American spirit. The heroic exploits of the frontier loom large in our consciousness, and our yearning to share somehow in that heritage is a persistent one.

Yet for the corporate man of the 1970s, bound to a career behind a desk or on the assembly line, the hardships and perils of the frontier life often seem distant indeed. Only in our spare time are most of us able to satisfy our need to identify with the heroic myths. Most do it vicariously, savoring the larger-than-life heroics of fictional private eyes and TV gunslingers or rooting for the football warriors who gather for battle on Sunday afternoons. Others take a more direct approach, dashing off on weekends to climb mountains, race motorcycles, jump from airplanes or otherwise risk life and limb in satisfaction of the aching need for adventure.

But there are still some men who needn't look beyond their own workaday routines to find the excitement that others restlessly pursue in their spare time. These men have jobs that, even in this institutional era, demand that the individual put his personal skill and courage to the test every time he goes to work.

This book is about such men. In it you will meet people like Don Sheldon, an Alaskan bush pilot whose daring rescue flights onto Mt. McKinley, the highest peak in North America, are legendary. And Tom West, an affable ironworker from Illinois who admits that part of the lure of scampering around the steel skeleton of an unfinished skyscraper is that "I like being able to do something that scares the hell out of other people."

There are articles, too, about a professional diver, a rodeo cowboy, a police patrol team and others whose jobs expose them regularly to danger. The articles, all of which appeared originally in The Wall Street Journal, explore some of the motives that lead men to such lives and some of the rewards they find.

They also explore the attitudes that make it possible for men to believe they can defy death day after day and still survive. The key lies, perhaps, in the calm self-confidence expressed by an Air Force captain attached to a crew that specializes in flying into hurricanes. "It's really not that dangerous if you do it the right way," the captain says. "And we do it the right way."

—JOHN BARNETT
Editor

Contents

Living Dangerously

Alaska Flier

WITH a raucous whine, the single-engine ski-equipped plane pierces the moonless night. Nearly 40 minutes and 90 miles of wilderness away from Anchorage, the runway lights of an airstrip clearly emerge in the blackness.

"We'll take the other runway—for convenience sake," casually comments the pilot, Don Sheldon. He veers away from the inviting lights and noses the small plane down in a dark void. "Hope there's no moose," he chuckles. The plane's skis gently touch down on what turns out to be another snowy runway amid a cluster of cabins. "We missed the big ones," the pilot advises, referring to potholes rather than moose, who have kept their distance. He taxis the plane to the door of a yellow and brown house located smack in the middle of "Beautiful Downtown Talkeetna," as a nearby sign informs.

Donald Edward Sheldon, one of Alaska's most celebrated bush pilots, is home. It has been a routine run—not like the time the left wing of his plane folded back at 1,500 feet. "They don't fly very well with one wing," he explains. The plane spun groundward and crashed—fortunately, in a clump of trees. The impact, though, destroyed the craft, knocking off the engine and folding the other wing. "I was upside down, drowning in gas," Don recalls. "So I kicked open the door and jumped. But I didn't realize I was so high." He tumbled 40 feet to the ground and walked away.

Or the time he helped deliver a baby on a flight to

Anchorage, one of the few births ever recorded in a single-engine plane. The problems were more mechanical than physical. A radio operator was relaying advice from a physician, but at times the transmissions were garbled so Don didn't always get the directions straight. Eventually, though, the details were clarified, and mother and child did fine.

Or the time Don hit a stump and broke a ski on a takeoff with three ministers as passengers. To land again, the ministers had to hang out the door in human-chain fashion in order that one of them could hold the damaged ski in place.

Lithe and wiry, 49-year-old Don Sheldon belongs to a brash breed who challenge, in flimsy flying machines, some of the world's most volatile weather and desolate terrain. Since the early 1920s, Alaska's bush pilots—they number about 700 now—have tenuously linked together this far-flung land mass where 300,000 people are scattered over 586,000 square miles.

Even today, roads and trails in Alaska total a mere 6,800 miles. Hence it's up to the pilots to service homesteaders, miners, trappers, hunters, fishermen, mountain climbers and others with essentials and occasional luxuries, ranging from dogsleds and dynamite to tobacco and tomatoes. Bush pilots will land almost anywhere—on sand bars, glaciers, rivers, ice floes, beaches, lakes, pastures, graveyards or ball fields. They face the constant danger that each landing may be their last.

In a retrospective book about bush pilots, Harmon Helmericks, himself a part-time Alaskan bush pilot, writes that "none of the pilots ever got rich, most of them went broke eventually, a very few made it all the way through and were able to retire modestly, some drifted into other fields—but most of them died trying." Any exaggeration is slight. Two historians recently compiled a list of the top 100 bush pilots from Alaska's past; at least 25 had been killed in air crashes.

Bush pilots like Don Sheldon, naturally, are better off than their predecessors. Planes have been improved. Powerful radios and radar help. Mr. Sheldon can even phone 24 hours a day and hear a continually updated weather report based on data from a Tiros satellite. But the untamed combination of climate and country still exacts its toll in the nation's flyingest state.

About one Alaskan in 40 is a licensed pilot, compared with about one in 300 for the nation as a whole. Ten percent of all Federal Aviation Agency flight service stations are in Alaska. That state is also the only place where the FAA had to erect a flight tower alongside a lake solely for float planes.

The state, with less than 0.25% of the nation's population, accounted for about 4% of the 1,270 deaths in small-plane accidents investigated in 1970 by the National Transport Safety Board. It isn't unusual for military and Civil Air Patrol planes to be searching for four or five missing planes at one time. In fact, one FAA official, only half kidding, wonders whether that isn't the military's main mission in Alaska. "They seem to spend all their time doing it," he says.

Don Sheldon, who has been on both sides of rescue missions, hasn't escaped injuries. In more than 22 years of bush flying, he has had 44 planes, three of which were "totaled" in accidents. He sustained his most serious injuries, however, on a steep glacier in Alaska's rugged Wrangell Mountains, some 16 miles from where he had landed. He was on foot, guiding two wealthy bankers through the mountains, when he spotted a sheep traversing a possible shortcut over the glacier, a six-inch-wide shale ridge. "If sheep could cross it, I could, too," he says. But halfway across he was caught in a rock-and-snow slide and swept 400 feet down the glacier before "I collided with a rock outcropping that I managed to hang onto."

With rope, the bankers pulled him to safety, and he began his most painful journey, 16 miles back to the plane with a broken right shoulder and a body covered with cuts, abrasions and bruises. To avoid blacking out, he had to rest every three or four steps. "It seemed like 1,600 miles," he grimaces. One of the bankers, a licensed pilot, then flew the plane out.

Don is an exuberant soul whose conversations turn into far-ranging monologues. In one long breath, he may skip from an unsolved 30-year-old murder in Talkeetna to the Japanese method of making green tea to a dissertation on Alaskan game management. "He's crazy like Casey Stengel," says another highly talkative bush pilot who remembers he couldn't say a single word during a flight with Don. "He's always got five ideas working at once."

Don Sheldon was born in Colorado, drifted as a Depression-reared teen-ager from a logging camp in Wyoming to peach-picking in Washington to driving a milk wagon in Anchorage and, in August 1938 at the age of 17, to Talkeetna, in the bush north of Anchorage. "With gold in the summer and fur in the winter, it was a booming town," he reminisces. "Everyone burned wood, and the town smelled like a big bonfire mixed with booze fumes."

For a living, he tried his hand at chopping firewood, gold mining (50 cents an hour for a 10-hour shift, seven days a week) and skinning beavers (his first took him two days to skin—"They're hard to skin if you don't know how"). Subsequently, he attended the University of Alaska in Fairbanks for a semester and joined a survey team traveling around Alaska (in his first big job, he laid out some sewer lines backwards). All the while, he was rubbing elbows with the folk heroes of the day —daredevil bush pilots who barnstormed the territory in ancient planes almost literally stuck together with baling wire and spit. He was permanently inflicted with a mania to fly.

"I looked at them like something from Mars," Don says. "I could also tell at a glance that it was the way to get around the country."

The results were flying lessons in late 1941, a hitch in the Air Corps as a tail gunner during World War II, a postwar course in a mechanics' school and the decision in the spring of 1948 to return to Alaska. "My mind must have been paralyzed with frost, and when spring came, it thawed," he figures.

He linked up with a businessman-flyer named Stub Morrison, and they went into the bush-pilot business. (In 1951, Mr. Morrison was killed in one of Alaska's most treacherous weather conditions, radiation fog. That's when a slight drop in the temperature causes a blanket of fog to fall in a matter of seconds. "He just flew into the ground," Don says.)

Don settled in Talkeetna (population about 100) when old friends threw him some business. Even so, he was reduced to shooting wolves from his plane to collect bounties of $50 apiece to make ends meet. But the Talkeetna location proved propitious.

Looming some 75 miles from the town, a short hop in this country, is the majestic Alaska range, crowned by 20,320-foot Mt. McKinley, the highest peak in North America. During the 1950s, Don handled the flying for a survey of the rugged range by Bradford Washburn, an explorer and director of the Boston Museum of Science. The survey not only opened the range to mountain climbers but produced increasingly lucrative business for Don, who had his own intimate knowledge of the range and Mt. McKinley. He staked out an almost exclusive franchise to Mt. McKinley. This past year, he serviced 18 separate climbing expeditions, a personal record.

"I don't claim McKinley as my own, but I did get in on the ground floor," he says. "I can negotiate the winds, the snow and the geography." He's being uncharacteristically modest. A close friend avers that "he truly believes it's his mountain." And a one-time passenger remembers his spotting the wreckage of a plane on the mountain's slopes and quipping, "He tried to outbid me."

Don's expertise was put to a stern test in 1960. Two separate expeditions climbing Mt. McKinley ran into trouble. In one, a woman was near death in a coma, while four climbers in the other were injured in a fall. Relying on thermal drafts to force his plane to altitudes it couldn't reach on its own, Don made repeated airdrops of supplies at 17,000 feet. But getting the climbers off the mountain was another matter.

Mr. Washburn, calling from Boston, conferred with his old friend and mentioned a possible landing site at 14,200 feet, higher than any plane had ever set down on the mountain. Don found the spot—a steep, hidden plateau—and negotiated a tricky, dangerous landing as well as a rendezvous with the sick woman. For the next four days and nights, he was in the air almost constantly, making landing after landing. In the end, he plucked 18 people off the slopes.

His rescues are almost legendary. One involved eight Army scouts who were to explore a stretch of wild river rushing through appropriately named Devil's Canyon. Don happened to be in the neighborhood, so he thought he'd check them out. What he found was six of the eight clinging to the sheer wall of the canyon. "They were almost through when a whirlpool smashed their boat against the wall," he relates.

Landing upstream, he let his float-equipped plane, under full power, drift backwards down the river. The idea: to pick them off the wall. With waves as high as his wings, "it took me about five passes before I got the first guy," he says. "My wings, too, were inches from the canyon wall." One by one, he pulled them into the plane, then backed down the river a mile and a half through white water until he could turn around and take off. He also rescued the other two scouts. One was washed up on an island while the other was floating down the river on a piece of wreckage.

On another occasion, he joined a search in a blinding snowstorm for a missing Air Force C47 with 16 men aboard. From the air, he spotted what he thought were bloody moose tracks and, despite the storm, he managed to follow the tracks. Instead of moose, he came upon three of the plane's six survivors. "The plane had broken up in the air at 10,000 feet, and, unbelievably, the six had lived to tell about it," he says.

Officially, Don Sheldon operates the Talkeetna Air Service. Except for a part-time pilot during the busy summer season, the concern consists of Don and his young wife, Roberta. "If we were a government agency, we'd have 10 people here," laughs Mrs. Sheldon. While her husband functions as pilot, as mechanic and even as clerk filling grocery orders for bush customers, Mrs. Sheldon is the bookkeeper, secretary, radio operator and "a good trouble shooter." She used to fly, but gave it up when they married.

Mrs. Sheldon is the daughter of Robert Reeve, one of Alaska's most famous bush pilots. The 68-year-old Mr. Reeve, who doesn't fly any longer, operates Reeve

Aleutian Airways Inc., a 12-plane scheduled carrier serving the Aleutian Islands. During his courtship, Don plied Roberta's father with pungent moose sausage and caribou meat, prompting the old flier to crack that he wasn't losing a daughter but saving a liver. The Sheldons were married in May 1964, and their honeymoon featured one of Don Sheldon's rare plane mishaps.

In a plane decorated with pink toilet paper, they flew to a frozen lake in the bush and a cabin borrowed from a friend. The next morning, they discovered the ice thawing and the plane's right ski at a dangerous tilt. "If it thawed more, it could plunge right through," Mrs. Sheldon says. That's precisely what happened when Don tried to move it. He had to radio for two friends, who flew out and helped him pull the plane out of the water with a block and tackle.

"Don was real embarrassed," Mrs. Sheldon confides. "He had kept preaching never to go near the outlets of a lake during the spring thaw. They never let him forget it."

Today, the ruddy bush pilot flies five single-engined planes—three six-seat Cessna 180s, a Cessna 185 specially equipped for shorter takeoffs and landings, and a two-seat Piper Supercub. (Many bush pilots shun multiengined craft. "It's hard enough to keep one engine warm and going," Don huffs.) The Supercub is for tight, marginal landings, while each of the Cessnas is equipped with different landing gears—wheels, skis and floats—to handle any job.

In 1965, Don committed himself to paying $100,000 plus interest for four of the planes. (He just bought the Cessna 185 recently.) "Roberta said if I ever did it again, she'd leave me," he says. At the same time, he offered $50,000 to buy out the company's interest held by the widow of his former partner. "We just got it all paid off," he says proudly. "I didn't know if I could do it, but I did" by grossing $340,000 during the five-year period. "That's a lot of dough for a one-horse outfit like ours."

This past year, he grossed about $70,000, charging $60 an hour for flying the Cessnas and $40 an hour for the Supercub. "If I don't fly at least 1,000 hours a year, we haven't had much of a season," he says. His flying is heavily concentrated in the summer, when the Alaskan sun not only warms the chilly clime, but stays out for much of the day. "He has tremendous endurance," says Roberta Sheldon. "He'll work from 5 a.m. to 1 a.m. and only get three or four hours sleep. In this business, you've got to make a living in the summer season. And if you have a week of bad weather and traffic piles up, you have to really fly to get that revenue in."

To a close friend, known as "Evil" Alice Powell, "Don's a fine pilot and he works hard. In fact, I think he pushes himself too hard. But that's why he makes money and many others don't." Mrs. Powell, who got her nickname from the shady ladies in the brothels she inspected as a sanitation officer during territory days, runs a motel-restaurant in Talkeetna and arranges bush trips. "Don's dependable, too," she says. "If I have someone, I don't have to pull Don off a bar stool somewhere. He never touches a drop."

With the cutthroat competition, the economics of bush flying can be as tricky as the flying itself. Along with the costs of planes and maintenance, for example, Don had to shell out $1,800 for a base radio as well as nearly $400 apiece for eight mobile units he sets up at the camps of mountain climbers. "We also keep a lot of sleeping bags, coats and other gear for people who show up at the door unprepared," Mrs. Sheldon says. More important, though, is insurance.

Like most bush pilots, Don can't even afford to insure his planes. In three years, he grumbles, premiums for the so-called hull insurance would equal the price of the plane. He must carry passenger liability insurance, but its price has been soaring. In 1970, he paid $7,000 in premiums to Lloyds of London, which covers Alaskan aviation, up from $5,300 in 1969 and $2,500 in 1968.

Mrs. Sheldon, who handles the books, blames crashes by heavy aircraft on the oilrich, remote North Slope for the steep increases. "I wrote them myself, pointing out that he never had a fatality," she laments. "He knows his limitations in marginal weather, and he overhauls his engines before they're due. I brought up all these things, but it didn't do any good. It's another case of the little man paying the brunt because of the big guys. You can cry about it but you can't change it."

(Attesting to the perilous nature of the job, bush pilots must also pay 35% to 75% extra merely to insure themselves, according to a major insurance company. Commercial jet pilots, on the other hand, pay the same as a stockbroker or any ordinary businessman.)

The most serious injury suffered by a Talkeetna Air Service passenger, Don says, occurred 20 years ago when a tricky wind presented him with the choice of riding his plane into a cliff or flipping it into a lake. He chose the lake. The passenger, he says, emerged from the crash with "a big bump on his head. He figured this was it. But after a couple shots of booze, he was on his feet again."

The plane, however, was lost. To this day, Don forlornly calls that lake "8G lake," short for eight grand, or $8,000, the price of the lost plane.

Don doesn't like to talk about the dangers of bush flying. "I'm still around after 28 years of flying, so it must be relatively safe," he says. Everyone faces dangers, he says. "You could be struck by a garbage truck in Anchorage." But he admits that few of the buddies he had when he began flying are still around. The job, he says, permits him to sate his desires to fly, make hundreds of friends all over Alaska and "to produce a memory" that will linger after he's gone. He disdainfully dismisses commercial jet pilots with two words: "taxi drivers."

His wife, having grown up in a bush pilot's family, says the bush pilots "take the consequences of the danger to do what they like to do. It's just something in their blood. It's a drive in itself. Both Dad and Don have it. And if your husband is going to be happy, it's most important that he better be doing what he likes." Don, she says, "is such a competent fellow that every time I get frightened, a little voice says, 'Don't worry.' " Yet she notes how he continually "risks his life to protect those kooky climbers" and adds somewhat wistfully, "Why, when he has so much here, would he do things like that?"

With their two young daughters, the Sheldons live quietly in Talkeetna, now a way station along the federally owned Alaska Railroad. "All we talk about is how lucky we are to live here, with the peace and solitude," she says. "We're only 35 or 40 miles from the city, too. Some people drive that long to work every day."

When Don isn't catching up on his sleep ("He hibernates a lot in the winter," Mrs. Sheldon says), his rare spare time may be spent collecting driftwood, picking berries with his daughters, dabbling with watercolors, making furniture or preparing some moose jerky in a smokehouse he recently built.

Though he used to shoot wolves for their bounty, Don now limits his hunting to a very occasional moose for the larder. The years of flying have transformed him into an ardent conservationist, even to the point where he will only rarely take out a hunter. With his mood shifting between outrage and sadness, he talks about the vast stretches of vacant bush that once teemed with wildlife, and about spotting piles of white fox and other animals who died from eating poison ostensibly left out for wolves. At present, he's campaigning against a State Fish and Game Department proposal to expand the hunting season on antlerless moose. "It's subversive," he charges. "They don't want to be control agents. They want to destroy what we pay them to protect."

In the pioneer days of bush flying, the wives often went days without a word from their husbands. But Roberta Sheldon stays in constant radio contact with Don, an arrangement that isn't always a comfort. Not long ago, Don flew to rescue a dying climber at 15,000 feet in the Alaska Range. Back at home, his wife received word the climber had died and to call off the mission. "But I couldn't get hold of him, though I could hear him," she says. "For some reason, he hadn't taken his oxygen and I could tell he was getting giddy. I was really scared." Fortunately for Don, turbulent winds forced him to return without attempting a landing.

Don has had closer shaves. Flying near the town of Wainwright, above the Arctic Circle, he was engulfed by a whiteout, a feared condition peculiar to the region. He likens it to flying in a bowl of milk. Light filtering through a cloud cover becomes equal to the light reflected off the snow, blotting out the horizon as well as the pilot's ability to discern land from air. Only dark objects can be seen.

"I was good and disgusted until I caught sight of a friendly shoreline," he says. It was a ridge of ice more than 100 feet high. He followed it and, just as suddenly, lost sight of it. "I was really sweating it," he allows.

Then his passenger, a fur buyer, caught sight of a red fox. "It looked like it was going up our right wing."

They were actually flying below and precariously close to the ridge. Don gained altitude and began searching for a caribou herd. During whiteouts, caribou give pilots some perspective and also an indication that the land probably is flat and landable. He did spy what he took to be grazing caribou. "I just landed," he laughs, "and nearly ran over an old Eskimo and his 10 dogs."

On another flight, he became lost in a surprise storm with his fuel running low. He landed on a steep, snowy incline of a peak 170 miles southwest of Mt. McKinley, it turned out, and immediately a widespread air search was launched for him. He had to tip up the tail of his plane to drain the last drops of gas forward to keep his radio sending a signal ("It was a helluva job") and he had to continually beat down 2,000 feet of snow for a takeoff. "The snow, you wouldn't believe it," he says. "Eight feet of new snow fell. Flakes were bigger than $200 bills. I was there five days, but it seemed like a month. There's a lot of planes lost and never recovered."

He stacked wood in three piles for signal fires, to be lit with the fluid in his engine heater. Just before his radio died, he heard the whir of a plane in the sky. "I rushed to those three tremendous piles of scrub timber, but they didn't burn like any timber I had seen. They just went poof, with little puffs of smoke. There were my three tremendous bonfires."

In desperation, he took off his engine cover and frantically began waving it. It worked. Air drops of gas then permitted him to finish his flight.

These scrapes don't faze him, and they don't

prompt any talk about retiring. "I don't care to quit," he vows. "I'd rather wear out than rust."

But some Alaskans think the whole bush pilot fraternity is a dying one. Scheduled jets now connect points that once were the private domain of the bush pilot. People are increasingly clustering in the larger towns. New highways are opening bush country once accessible only by plane. Homesteaders, miners and trappers are themselves vanishing. Even noisy snowmobiles, a proliferating phenomenon in Alaska, are allowing people to get off the beaten path.

However, as Roberta Sheldon puts it: "We'll always have Mt. McKinley. You can't build a highway up that mountain. We figure that's his ace in the hole."

—JAMES E. BYLIN

Combat Cameraman

WHEN Keith Kay goes off to war, he seems singularly unprepared for survival on the battlefield. He carries no weapons. Instead, he lugs a bulky 30-pound movie camera that makes it hard for him to run or duck and in itself presents a fat target to snipers. He usually doesn't wear a steel helmet because it would block the viewfinder of his camera. When the shooting starts and everybody else dives for cover, Keith can't—not if he wants to do his job.

Keith is a television news cameraman, and his job is to cover the war in Indochina. That means he spends much of his time taking films of combat—something he can't do lying on his belly in a ditch or behind a mound of dirt. "You can lie behind two feet of dirt and take notes or talk into a mike, but you can't take film through two feet of dirt," observes Jeff Gralnick, a CBS producer who has worked in Vietnam.

Covering the Indochina war has proven to be hazardous for all types of reporters and photographers. The latest casualty count is 34 newsmen and women dead and 17 missing since 1965. But it's widely agreed that the TV cameraman, because of his heavy gear and his need to film continuous stretches of action, is probably the most vulnerable.

For 27-year-old Keith Kay, the hazards have become almost routine. He has covered the war off and on since 1963 and has been in Saigon for most of 1968 through 1971, first as a CBS staff cameraman and later as a free lance with regular assignments from CBS. He filmed the early American advisory effort, went through the big battles of 1967-68—Con Thien, Dak To, Khe Sanh and Tet—and is recording the dreary lives and deaths of American GIs during the limbo months of the U.S. withdrawal.

His combat coverage in 1967 won him an Emmy award—the TV industry's highest accolade—and he was part of the broadcasting team that was nominated for another Emmy in 1971 for "The World of Charlie Company," a CBS news special first broadcast during the summer of 1970. Keith and the other members of the "Charlie Company" team have won the Overseas Press Club's 1971 George Polk Memorial Award, which recognizes "the best reporting in any medium requiring exceptional courage and enterprise abroad."

At times during 1969 and 1970, Keith has left Indochina to cover news stories elsewhere for CBS. Inevitably, it seems, these stories have contained their own elements of violence and danger—rioting in Mexico City, war in Biafra, conflict in the Middle East, student rioting back home in the States. Working out of his home base in Hong Kong, Keith is back in Indochina.

Keith's personal habits, to the very limited extent they can be separated from his job, are probably a bit livelier than those of most Americans. He races motorcycles and scuba dives; he wears bell-bottomed pants and lets his prematurely grey hair droop over his collar; he chain-smokes Camels and sometimes puffs on stronger stuff; he eats often and indiscriminately, everything from C-rations to dried cuttlefish. But when he's home in Hong Kong he spends most of his time with his wife, Michele, and their daughter, Deborah, listening to music, studying tropical fish and laying plans for a Japanese rock garden he wants to build in his living room.

Keith says he doesn't see himself as an adventurer. Being a cameraman is his profession, and the danger isn't something he seeks. It is simply part of the job, and through experience and common sense he tries to minimize the risks as much as possible.

Keith grew up in the Far East, the son of a foreign correspondent. He spent a year and a half at college in the U.S. studying forestry ("It was as good as any other training for photography") and then went off to Vietnam as a still photographer in 1963. A year later, shuffling around in the rubble of a blown-up Saigon building, he heard an ABC correspondent cursing the fact that he lacked a cameraman. Keith volunteered to fill in, neglecting to say he had never operated a TV camera before. But he managed.

His new career was soon interrupted, however, by the U.S. Army, which drafted Keith in Saigon and then sent him to New York for a two-year tour. Out of the Army, he returned to Vietnam as a free-lance photographer and in 1967 was hired by CBS as a staff cameraman. (A network cameraman in Indochina generally works with a correspondent and a soundman, who is attached to the cameraman by a kind of umbilical cable of wires connecting their equipment.)

Keith began to make a name for himself during the 1967 fighting around the Marine base of Con Thien. He was working with CBS correspondent Jack Laurence, who became his closest friend and was his usual partner for two years of the war. "Jack kind of discovered Con Thien, though it later became a journalistic tourist attraction," says Keith. Jack, Keith and a soundman made the trip into Con Thien a dozen times, riding in truck and tank convoys that were invariably ambushed by dug-in North Vietnamese troops.

Keith remembers Con Thien as "incredible—sitting

in Con Thien was like watching a war movie. I mean, people had been going on operations in Vietnam for years, but this was war as you imagined war. Not just walks in the sun through the paddies.

"We'd be sitting on a bunker watching a battalion go across a field below and suddenly the NVA rockets started coming into them and they would scatter across the field. . . . There was a lot of shell shock at Con Thien, things happening to peoples' minds, things no one had seen before in the war. We tried to capture the people and the place on film."

Recording the feeling or mood of a place and the thoughts and emotions of its people—particularly the American combat infantryman or "grunt"—became a specialty with Jack and Keith. Among all the carnage and courage that Keith filmed at Con Thien, one small scene sticks with him: "This medic was sitting on a bunker putting on a pair of clean white socks. All around him was the mud and the dirt and the shell craters. Jack just walked up to him and started rapping, 'Hey, what are you doing', and the Marine started talking about his socks and the mud and his life. It was natural, and it said something about Con Thien and men and war."

But, of course, what Keith calls "people stories" also were often combat stories—an inevitable situation with more than 1,000 mortar rounds landing on Con Thien each day. "We just inevitably wound up getting the bang-bang stuff. We'd be filming something else and shells would come in and start exploding on the camera frame. There was no particular skill or courage involved in it. But (CBS News headquarters in) New York was impressed."

Khe Sanh, the Marine base near the Laotian border that was besieged for two months in early 1968, was to most journalists, as to those Marines involved, the worst bit of hell the Vietnam war produced. The most dangerous part about Khe Sanh was getting in or out on cargo planes loaded with ammunition or fuel, flying through NVA .50-caliber machinegun fire and racing across the runway as mortar rounds slammed in. Planes wouldn't even come to a complete stop on the Khe Sanh strip before taking off again. Even some of the most veteran war correspondents considered one trip to Khe Sanh one too many.

Keith went into Khe Sanh six times, usually staying there several days at a stretch. "I'd had some experience by then, but I was spooked by Khe Sanh. It was harder getting out of bed in the morning in Khe Sanh when you knew you were leaving the place. One day there were 34 guys in a bunker just off the airstrip and the first 30 got killed or wounded trying to reach a plane. And they were going in groups of three or four. There were grunts who had been in Khe Sanh for three months and who would pass up a leave rather than risk that run from the bunker to the plane. It was the most frightening thing in Vietnam, and we had to do it every couple of days. . . . I remember sitting in a plane on the Khe Sanh strip listening to the mortars come in, clump, clump, clump, and I was watching peoples' faces. There was this one GI who was trying to whistle, only no sound would come out. But I'd like to have seen my own face."

Keith recalls filming a group of Marines sitting on a bunker singing "Where Have All the Flowers Gone." "The mist was coming in over those green hills and it was somehow even beautiful." But there usually wasn't time to film an uninterrupted scene like that. "Mortar rounds kept coming in, and I would duck or the guys I was filming would duck and so heads were always disappearing from the frame. It was great psychedelic film."

By far the bloodiest chapter of the Vietnam war was the Communist Tet offensive of February 1968. Keith covered it from the snipers in Saigon's slums to the battles in the streets of Hue.

"It was another new experience, street fighting," he says. "At Hue we slept on the floor of the American compound. In the morning Jack would mix some coffee, a C-ration breakfast, and then we'd go off to work. You only had to walk two blocks to where grunts were smashing in doors and spraying machinegun fire. You could be back at the compound for coffee at 11. The war was just there, whenever you wanted it."

Jack and Keith spent much of their time in Hue filming one squad that was advancing through the city block by block. "It took them three days to cross one street, and when they finally made it there was just another block of NVA. Another day we had about 20 fences to cross, and I came to one and said, 'This is it, no more'. Jack said, 'Come on, just one more fence'. I said, 'We could get killed crossing one more fence'. And just then a bullet came in and hit a pole just behind Jack's head. We didn't cross that fence."

"You get those hunches sometimes," says Keith. But unlike some other correspondents, Keith has no faith in lucky hats or charms. "I'm afraid to. If I ever lost my good-luck charm I might also lose my mind."

Luck no doubt has a good deal to do with staying alive in Vietnam. But so does experience and judgment. "In the early days of the war, out of inexperience, I sometimes found myself the only one standing up in a firefight," Keith says. "By being stupid you can make a quick reputation of being brave. But later I started ducking quicker than GIs."

Keith acknowledges that a cameraman makes a bit

better target than anyone else, but he claims the odds of emerging from combat unscathed are still pretty good. "Say you're with a company that gets into a firefight. That's 120 men, and it's very rare to have more than five or six guys killed." And in a situation like that Keith doesn't worry much about classic camera technique. You do what you can. You don't worry about a steady camera and continuity and all those things students are taught. You just let yourself react to the action, and you get better film."

The Indochina war, of course, isn't all Con Thiens, Khe Sanhs and Hues. In Cambodia, for instance, a correspondent may spend many, many uneasy hours driving down insecure roads with nothing dramatic to show for it when he ends up back at Phnom Penh's Hotel Royal pool in the evening. In Vietnam, for every big battle there are hundreds of small engagements that may not make news even if a TV crew happens to be there. And for every hour a TV cameraman spends in the field he usually spends many more hours trying to get there, including hours and days wasted sitting in the dust on some military base waiting for a helicopter or a C-130 transport plane.

"It's kind of like commuting from Greenwich," says Keith. "You're sitting on the Dong Ha chopper pad with your Stars and Stripes under your arm and you meet a friend coming in from Khe Sanh. You share a can of C-rations and say, 'See you for a drink tonight in Danang.'" Then too, of course, there are the days or even weeks a cameraman spends hanging around Saigon or Danang waiting for some action to cover, times when Keith says his greatest danger is getting cirrhosis of the liver from drinking too much.

One of Keith's most unpleasant, and unproductive, experiences in Vietnam was a story on the Vietnamese

air force. This involved accompanying the pilots on bombing runs in their A-1 Skyraiders. On his first run Keith vomited all over the plane. On later runs he just vomited into plastic bags. In all he spent several weeks trying to film the story. "It got so bad no pilot wanted to take me. And the film I finally got was the most unexciting I ever took. The planes would go into their dives and I would tilt the camera down, down, down, and I always ended up with spectacular shots of my lap."

The only time Keith was injured in Indochina, and then only slightly, was while covering a Buddhist demonstration in Saigon in 1968. Some Vietnamese police were beating a girl with clubs and Keith began to film the scene. Then the police started beating Keith.

He finally made his escape in a hijacked cyclo (a kind of motorcyle-drawn cart), beating the driver over the head with his camera while the police chased after them waving clubs.

For several years Keith and Jack had been thinking of ways to expand their "people stories" into an in-depth look at the life of an average group of infantrymen. In the spring of 1970 CBS gave them the chance. The result was "Charlie Company," the celebrated documentary that, Keith says, "just tried to show the boredom of it all, your sons walking along through that jungle day after day." To capture this on film, the crew spent 37 nights with Charlie Company in the jungles of War Zone C. The crew shared and recorded the danger and the drudgery, the GI's private joys—like the sight of a mail sack dropped in by chopper—and the GI's daily agonies of ennui, fatigue and jungle rot.

There was some drama, too. At one point some of the GIs refused an order from a new company commander to walk down a road they thought was too dangerous. This "revolt," and the wide attention it got after it appeared on CBS, was actually disappointing to Keith, who felt the momentary drama detracted from the main theme—the very lack of drama much of the time in war.

To film Charlie Company, the crew generally spent five days and nights in the field, then five days out to resupply, ship their film and get a bit of rest. Then back to the field again, where Keith had to carry about 120 pounds of equipment, food, water and other supplies for eight hours a day of jungle hiking.

Charlie Company was satisfying personally as well as professionally. "We made lasting friendships with some of the men in that company," Keith says. "They could be killers, but they could also be the nicest, most compassionate guys in the world. It was the only commune I ever saw that really worked."

Keith's greatest frustration in filming Charlie Company came when he was dropped off in a jungle landing zone to spend a five-day stretch with the men, only to find that his camera was broken. There was nothing to do but carry the heavy, useless equipment until the next chopper came in five days later. This is another occupational problem for cameramen. A reporter always has his pen and note pad, or at least his memory. But a cameraman is dependent on a machine—though Keith says a camera is "nothing more important than a typewriter is to a writer, just a mechanical thing through which I can do and tell what I want." Another problem is moving a story once it's on film. A reporter can generally find some fast way to file a breaking story: Telex or cable or telephone. But film must be shipped at least as far as the nearest satellite broadcasting station. Keith, like other TV men, has seen good film die for want of a helicopter or jetliner.

For all the equipment and supplies Keith carries into the field, down to a portable tape recorder and canned peaches, one thing he never carries is a weapon. "We are supposed to be noncombatants," he says. Thus, while Keith was willing to help Charlie Company dig foxholes, he did not help the men set up mines.

Keith says he tries to avoid getting personally involved in the war. "If you get emotionally involved it can destroy you. You have to try and see the dead bodies and the ugliness as part of the landscape." But involvement can't always be avoided. Keith still vividly recalls, and regrets, an incident that happened several years ago when he was accompanying U.S. troops on a sweep of an enemy tunnel and bunker complex. Keith was walking alone when a Vietcong poked his head out of a nearby hole in the ground. Then out came the VC's hand, clutching a grenade. "I stared at him and shook my head, like to say no, just go back down into your hole. It seemed like we must have stared at each other for 15 seconds. Then out came his other hand with another grenade. So I yelled and dived into the brush, and some GIs came running over and dropped a grenade in the hole and killed him. I still feel bad about that. I keep wondering what the VC would have done if I hadn't yelled." (That experience is about as close as any correspondent is likely to get to a VC. Except as corpses or captives, the enemy is rarely seen, and then only as fleeting dark shadows in the brush.)

While Keith seeks to avoid personal emotional involvement in the war, he doesn't try and hide his general views on the conflict. "The war is definitely wrong and bad," he says. "But I feel that it is bad enough and wrong enough and ugly enough that I don't have to go out of my way to show it that way. I have never tried to prove it is bad. I just show the war like it is, and it tells itself." But if Keith opposes the war, he likes Vietnam and the Vietnamese and the American GIs. "I have a sort of love-hate relationship with Vietnam," he says.

Why does Keith continue to cover a war he opposes, which is destroying a country he likes and which could one day destroy him? "I don't know. Every time you go into combat I guess you find a different reason for it. You're looking for something in yourself or for something in others. And once you have seen men and their emotions in war, then everything else—Nixon, student radicals, Black Panthers, whatever—seems pretty staged. No one acts for a camera when he's under fire." Those are some of the reasons. So are friendships, which somehow seem closer in Vietnam than anywhere else. And so is the whole way of life to which Keith is attached.

Money is not a reason. When Keith worked as a CBS staff man in Vietnam in the most dangerous years of the war, he earned $300 a week. "I could have earned more in the States, with salary and overtime and extras. But in the States you end up working for the money instead of the profession. You might as well be an insurance salesman." Keith in fact did leave Vietnam in late 1968 and settled in San Francisco as an independent cameraman, which meant investing about $15,000 in a camera and other equipment (which an employer then rents from him when he takes an assignment). Working in the States, mostly on assignments for CBS, was profitable, with paychecks running up to $1,200 a week. But it wasn't Keith's sort of life, and so his stateside tour was mostly spent jetting from one world crisis to another.

Before long, he wound up back covering the war, and in 1970 he moved his family to Hong Kong. There his wife, Michele, tries not to think about what dangers Keith is facing when he's away from home.

"I don't mind his traveling as much as you would think," she says. "He goes crazy if he is home any length of time. He starts getting restless and pacing up and down, and I don't like to see that."

The thought of Keith being in danger "bothers me a lot," Michele adds. "But it bothered me most when I was living in the States, where I would see his stuff on TV and know that he was still out there and in danger. Living here in Hong Kong I usually don't know what he has done until it's over, which is better."

—PETER R. KANN

Bronc Rider

SHAWN Davis' workday begins when he eases himself down a narrow metal chute onto a seething bronco and mutters, "Okay, boys." It ends just a few seconds later when he is either pitched by the bucking horse or rescued by a mounted "pickup" cowboy after completing his ride.

Shawn's work is lucrative (he has made as much as $30,000 in a year totaling less than 15 minutes of riding), dangerous (he has broken his back, jaw and cheekbone and severed muscles in both upper legs) and exhausting (he's on the road 11 months a year).

Shawn is a professional rodeo cowboy, one of that daring breed of men who make their living riding wild broncos and bulls. And for Shawn Davis, a big man on the rodeo circuit despite his five-foot-eight-inch, 150-pound stature, it's a labor of love. "It's something that's a challenge always," he explains, a grin spreading across handsome features more appropriate to a movie star than a battered real-life cowboy. "You have great friendships, and you're free."

The 30-year-old Shawn is a champ, a likeable, tough-as-a-pineknot cowboy who's admired by fellow performers, pursued by pretty girls and applauded by rodeo crowds. Three times he has won the national championship for saddle bronc riding, and he wears a huge gold and copper oval belt-buckle attesting to his 1968 championship.

"A rodeo rider needs guts, and Shawn has more than his share of them," remarks David Stout, secretary-treasurer of the Rodeo Cowboys Association. "He seems mild-mannered, but the mild manner conceals a pretty tough interior."

Few rodeo riders seem to possess the right combination of guts, talent and luck. The Cowboys Association, which licenses rodeo riders, reports that in 1970 only 10 cowboys made "in the vicinity" of $25,000 (top prizewinner Larry Mahan won more than $41,000). That's out of a total of more than 3,400 cowboy members and another 2,700 who ride in rodeos on working permits issued by the association.

Paradoxically, for all the violent, exciting moments in the arena, most of the typical day of the typical rodeo rider is slow-paced. Though some cowboys are multitalented competitors who enter a number of events, many—like Shawn—are specialists who limit themselves to one. Thus, except for the infrequent occasions when there's another rodeo close enough to commute to in the same day, Shawn's time is his own except for the few seconds he's in the saddle.

Shawn flies to his rodeo engagements in his own single-engine blue-and-white Beechcraft Bonanza. Skimming over the Texas flatlands en route to Houston and a big rodeo at the Astrodome, he flips to country music on the plane's radio. "Ya-ha," he whoops happily, tapping his hand against the plane's stick in rhythm to the music.

When he lands, Shawn checks into a motel (usually a second-class, relatively inexpensive one) where other rodeo performers also stay. Aside from companionship, the other cowboys also usually provide him rides to and from the arena since most have their own cars or pickup trucks.

A Mormon who doesn't drink or smoke and who frets about the caffeine in his Cokes, Shawn spends his evenings idly swapping yarns with other cowboys. His friends say this is something of a departure from the days prior to his courtship and marriage to a stunning airline stewardess. In his early bachelor days, Shawn was regarded as something of a swinger, and there was usually a pretty girl around to help him while away an evening.

Shawn sleeps late, not rising until around 10. Then he heads for a hearty breakfast with other cowboys. Typically, he downs a breakfast steak, two eggs, French fries, biscuits and fruit juice.

Shawn, who holds a college degree in education but long ago discarded the idea of teaching, is the son of an Irish rancher in Montana. (Shawn's name originally was spelled "Sean," but he changed it when his classmates in school kept mispronouncing it.) Shawn started riding rodeo calves at five, bulls at 14 and broncos at 15. Now, in his motel room, he prepares for his work like an athlete, doing push-ups, backbends and other exercises. He also puts his worn saddle on the floor and sits on it, limbering it up. Then, still hours before the rodeo is to begin, he dresses in brown and yellow striped jeans, a bright yellow shirt and his dusty black boots.

Shawn arrives at the Astrodome early, lugging his saddle. He checks a list on the wall outside the rodeo secretary's office to see what horse he has drawn. The horse is picked in a lottery prior to the rodeo. With luck, Shawn will get a "good" horse—one that bucks hard and thus gives the rider a chance to score more points for a skillful ride.

For a while, Shawn stands around joking with other cowboys and chatting with two pretty girls who come down from the stands to introduce themselves. Like the "groupies" who follow rock musicians, a number of girls usually are on hand at rodeos flocking after the better-known young cowboys. In this case, one of the girls candidly offers to spend the night with Shawn —an offer that he gently declines.

As the first events of the rodeo are about to get under way, Shawn carries his saddle over to the chute from which he will ride. He pulls on cobalt-blue chaps with white fringes and rubs them with resin on the inside of the thighs. Then he begins to work himself into a nervous state. "That way, I'm thinking and getting my adrenalin working," he says. By mount-up time he will be as taut as the girth of his saddle, his nerves and muscles as fine-tuned as those of the excited horse trying to throw him.

During the event just before saddle bronc riding, the horses are run into their narrow chutes. Shawn begins to saddle and bridle his horse, which firmly resists the bit. Finally, Shawn gets the equipment in place, and he sits on the edge of the chute waiting for his turn to come up. As his number is called, Shawn drops down onto the horse. Then the announcer's voice booms:

"And now, ladies and gentlemen, the three-time champ of the saddle bronc riders—Shawn Davis. The Aubrey, Texas, cowboy has the horse Cactus Jack."

A cowboy reaches down from the fence alongside the chute to yank tight the flank strap, a length of leather lined with sheepskin encircling the horse to rankle him and insure a spirited performance. Shawn whispers, "Okay, boys," and the gate is thrown open. Cactus Jack leaps out into the arena, an angry, snorting dark-brown form.

For nine frenzied seconds, Shawn rides the plunging horse, one hand firmly gripping the reins and the other sweeping the air. The powerfully built animal is dancing, bucking, kicking, seething, fighting to dislodge the rider from his back. But Shawn sticks, raking the horse's side with his spurs (a requirement if he is to score well) until a horn blows to signal the end of his ride. A pickup man gallops his horse alongside Cactus Jack, and Shawn reaches over to grasp the pickup man's saddle and lift himself free of the bronco. Another pickup man retrieves the horse.

During his ride, Shawn has been evaluated by two judges, each of whom gives him a score of from one to 50 for a possible total of 100. Twenty-five points rest on the quality of the ride and 25 on the caliber of the horse's bucking. For this ride, Shawn scores 72—a new high for the rodeo.

The ride over, Shawn quickly unsaddles his horse and hurries to a white pickup truck where three other cowboys await him. There's another rodeo in Lake Charles, La., three hours away, and Shawn has scheduled a ride there this evening—one of the rare occasions when such an arrangement is possible. He'll have to be back in Houston the next afternoon for another ride in the Astrodome.

The cowboys stop in Lake Charles for dinner and then drive to the small rodeo grounds, which seats about 4,600. The wooden railings and small-town atmosphere are in sharp contrast to the opulence of the Astrodome with its 45,000 seats, its air-conditioning and its huge electronic scoreboard.

For Shawn, it isn't a productive evening. His horse bucks badly, and he scores a poor 52. Immediately after the ride, he slips out of his chaps, grabs his saddle and heads for the pickup, which immediately takes off for Houston, arriving after midnight.

The financial affairs of a rodeo cowboy are uncertain, to say the least. Shawn, for example, is a leading contender for the $4,000 first prize in saddle bronc riding at the Houston rodeo after three rides. But on his last ride, he is thrown by his horse in the chute and doesn't score at all, so he ends up with only about $600 in prize money. Out of that, he has to pay his motel, eating and transportation expenses and a $60 entrance fee.

Most of the 70 rodeos he will attend in a year are smaller and offer smaller takes. The one in Lake Charles, where he collected nothing, offered slightly over $500 to the winning saddle bronc rider. Shawn says his largest single haul was in San Antonio in 1968, when he won $2,500 in a single eight-second ride. Laid up most of last year by his bad back, he only earned $7,500.

In addition to prize money, a champion cowboy can benefit to some extent from commercial promotions. Shawn's name is used by makers of boots, hats and Western clothes. The promotions only bring "a couple thousand dollars a year," he says, but as a result of them, "about the only things I buy in clothes are underwear and socks."

If the pay is uncertain, the danger is not. It's always there. Shawn broke his back in May 1969 at a small rodeo in Thompson Falls, Mont., when the horse he was riding flipped on top of him. He was 100 miles from the nearest hospital, and the ride took five hours because the ambulance ran out of gas.

He lay in the hospital for three months, then was put in a cast that kept him flat on his back for another two and a half months. During that time, he was wheeled around in a bed that was carried in a specially equipped bus.

"Something like that makes you realize how lucky you are just to get around," Shawn says now. "They told me I would never be able to ride again. Personally, I always thought I could."

Shawn went from doctor to doctor looking for one

who would help him ride again. He finally found one in Nebraska. "He said for me to pace myself, like a fighter," he recalls.

A year later, after a torturous progression of steps and despite a still-troublesome back, he was back in the saddle on a bronc.

Shawn has had many other spills in his years with the rodeo, although he says that "in comparison to what most of the fellows have had, I've had comparatively few injuries."

Four years ago, in Jamestown, N.D., a horse reared with him aboard, and he lost a stirrup. The horse made a sharp circle in front of a fence, and Shawn tried to jump to it for safety. In jumping he caught a spur on a strap and was jerked behind the horse. The horse kicked him in the chest and knocked him unconscious. He escaped without serious injury, however.

He wasn't quite that lucky at a rodeo in Mesquite, Texas, later that year. He had ridden his bareback horse (in those days he rode in more than one event) for the allotted period of time and was waiting for the pickup riders. His horse ran into a wet, soft spot in the arena floor at top speed, flipped and did a complete somersault, landing on Shawn. The impact whipped his head into the ground and broke his jaw.

For three weeks, Shawn's jaw was wired. Then he was fitted with a special plate, which he had to wear in his lower jaw for another six weeks. But with the plate, he could resume his life on the rodeo circuit.

In Red Bluff, Calif., Shawn was riding a bull that had been voted "bucking bull of the year" by the top 15 bull-riders. The angry bull jerked him down on its head, whipped him with its tail, threw him off and then kicked him in the ear. Shawn had fluid behind his ear drum for three weeks.

(Sometimes accidents are more embarrassing than

harmful. One cowboy was thrown by a horse into a high wire fence, where he hung upside down by his spurs until he could be rescued.)

Shawn has never been dragged by a horse ("I've been lucky in this respect," he says), although he has had some close calls. In Amarillo, Texas, some time ago, he caught his foot in the flank strap as he was jumping from his bronc onto the pickup horse. "I was just lucky the pickup man had ahold of the horse, or he would have dragged me till they caught him," he says.

"You have lots and lots of near accidents you don't pay any attention to," Shawn says. Why does he keep going back for more? "It's the challenge of the unknown," he explains. "Once you can do something quite well, it's hard to change, even though I know that someday I'll have to do something else."

His broken back left an impression on Shawn, even though it didn't scare him enough to give up rodeoing altogether. "I'm aware of the danger, but I'm not afraid of it like I was right after the accident," he says.

However, for Shawn's wife, Jeanna, who still works as a stewardess for Eastern Air Lines, the back injury was more traumatic. "I always thought nothing could happen to him until he broke his back," she says. "Now, I worry about it considerably. If he gets on a horse that rears, my heart sort of misses a beat."

For Shawn, and other cowboys like him, following the rodeo means a life largely away from home. During winter months, he's often home two or three days a week between rodeos. But during the summer, the peak season for rodeos, he may be away for months at a time.

Shawn lives with his wife and infant son, Zane Paul, in a spacious four-bedroom brick house in Aubrey, Texas, some 45 miles north of Dallas. His mantel is covered with three large riding trophies. The house, which he rents, is set on 130 acres of land, and horses and steers roam the property. When cowboys drop in for a visit, as they often do, they have roping contests in the corral in Shawn's backyard.

"Sometimes you would like to get home," he says, "but if you're home too long after being used to traveling for years, you get bored." Shawn says he enjoyed the traveling life prior to getting married. "I had enough friends there, and being with people is like being home." But he adds, "it has changed a bit since I've been married."

Shawn uses his travels to fit in his favorite sport outside of rodeos—skiing. He regularly skis when he's at the Denver rodeo early in the year, and he also does some skiing in California in the spring. However, he says, "it's difficult to get as much as I would like to."

Though rodeos enjoy widespread popularity in the United States, particularly in the West, they are roundly criticized by some people as being cruel to animals. The Humane Society of the United States, a Washington-based group, charged in a series of magazine and newspaper advertisements that horses become "bucking broncos" only when they are subjected to painful pressure from flank straps and poked with electric prods. "Without pain," the ads say, "there probably would not be any rodeo."

Shawn bristles at such charges. "If anyone is caught doing anything to a horse that might damage him," he says, "they'll throw you out of the rodeo, fine you and maybe suspend you for a time."

He adds: "That's the way it should be. Cowboys appreciate good bucking horses and their spirit. They have respect for them."

Says Mr. Stout of the Rodeo Cowboys Association: "These animals are valuable to the people who own them, and they're certainly not going to allow them to be mistreated. There's no question that we make every effort to see that they're not hurt."

This claim is generally supported by the American Humane Association, a national federation of humane societies from which the Humane Society of the United States broke off in 1954. Milton Searle, director of animal protection services for the American Humane Association, says his group works with the cowboys association to eliminate cruelty to rodeo animals, and "normally whatever corrective measures we ask for we get."

Mr. Searle adds: "We feel it's not the rodeo itself that's cruel—it's individuals within it that tend at times to be cruel."

Unlike the broncos of olden days, which were unbroken horses that had been roaming wild, the animals now used have been "spoiled" during breaking or are cantankerous by nature and are sold by ranchers to firms that provide them to rodeos.

Rodeo broncos lead a generally easy life compared to working ranch horses, cowboys maintain, and some of them have been on the rodeo circuit for 20 years.

That's longer than many cowboys last. Most of them are over the hill at 35, if not sooner. Shawn is making plans for that eventuality. He hopes to purchase some land (he already owns some real estate in California and Montana) to start a ranch for a summer camp for boys. "I'm really enthusiastic about the boys ranch," he says. "This is really what I'd like to do."

But for now, at least, he plans to continue battling broncos. He says, with a smile, "I still haven't completely worn myself out on rodeos."

—ERIC MORGANTHALER

Unruffled Officers

PATROLMAN Bob Brus of the New York Police Department draws his revolver, flicks on his flashlight and creeps gingerly up the dark, littered fire escape. The third stair below the second-floor landing is missing, and even with the light he almost steps into the gaping hole.

Reaching the top of the three-story building, part of a row of adjoining structures half a block west of Columbia University on Manhattan's Upper West Side, Officer Brus flashes the beam around the roof. A caller a few minutes earlier had reported a prowler on the fire escape, but the patrolman sees no one. As Officer Brus makes his way slowly back down the steps, another policeman a flight below peers toward the ground and barks: "Hey, who's that down there with the long sideburns? Oh, it's only Luzon."

Everybody chuckles, including Patrolman Jack Luzon, who has been searching the alley beneath the fire escape. The officers return to their radio cars and resume patrolling.

Not all searches for prowlers are so uneventful, especially these days. Most police checks of dark alleys or apartment hallways end just as that one near Columbia did—with a quip or two, and no culprit. But an alarming number of seemingly routine police calls in cities across the country lately have ended instead in violent death or injury to officers at the hands of snipers lying in wait or other armed individuals who choose to shoot rather than be searched or questioned.

Some of the slain or wounded officers have been shot as they tried to make routine arrests for such minor matters as traffic violations. These seemingly random attacks are bad enough. But even more upsetting to authorities have been obviously premeditated attacks that involved planting bombs in officers' cars or sniping at policemen from ambush.

The outbreak of snipings, in particular, appears to have clear racial overtones. Many—though by no means all—of the attacks have occurred in black ghetto neighborhoods and have been directed against white officers.

The snipings have occurred often in circumstances similar to Officer Brus's investigation of the building near Columbia University, which borders Harlem. Typically, a sniping incident begins with a routine-sounding telephone call to police about a prowler or a disorderly man in an apartment building—the sort of call to which the nation's police respond thousands of times each day. Having made or arranged the call, the sniper perches on a roof or in a window across the street from the building police have been asked to check. When the officers arrive and emerge from their cars into plain view, the sniper opens fire.

Theories on the reasons behind the attacks vary widely. Edward J. Kiernan, president of the Patrolmen's Benevolent Association, the 30,000-member New York City police union, calls the assaults "part of a coldly logical, hard-eyed revolutionary strategy . . . the direct result of inflammatory instruction by revolutionary groups." Mayor John Lindsay, however, said after conferring with New York police officials that investigations don't indicate the incidents in New York are related to each other or are part of a multi-city plot.

Surprisingly, some policemen don't appear worried about the growing threat of deadly surprise attacks. Patrolmen in New York and other cities are following a few new security procedures devised to deal with sniper attacks. But two evenings spent on patrol with Officer Brus and his colleagues in Harlem suggest that police officers tend to be fatalistic and even a bit flip about this threat, just as they are about other dangerous aspects of their jobs.

True, there's a lot of violent crime in Harlem, and the threat of assaults on police makes the situation even worse. But shooting or being shot at still is a rare experience for the individual cop who works there.

Patrolman Brus was one of the first officers at the scene of a sniping incident in Harlem early in 1970 in which two policemen were wounded. But in 11 years as a policeman in that section of the city he has never been shot at and has fired his gun only once.

Occasionally he investigates such crimes as a taxi robbery, a purse-snatching or a mugging, many of which involve dope addicts. But more often he finds himself quieting family squabbles, checking padlocks on abandoned buildings, helping disabled motorists, investigating water leaks or simply riding around waiting for calls about incidents that often aren't as serious as the caller had made it seem. Officer Brus sees far more situations that are ambiguous and require judgment and mediation than incidents that are clear-cut crimes demanding decisive police action.

So, much like the motorist who assumes he'll never be the one killed in a car accident, Bob Brus and most of his colleagues essentially depend on luck and the law of averages to get them through the few dangerous situations they may confront and spend very little time worrying about them.

"Sure, there's always a chance something will happen, but if you worry about it you'll go crazy," says Jack Luzon with a shrug, puffing one of the three or four cigarettes he smokes daily. Bob Brus agrees: "We're a little more cautious now, but basically being on the alert for these attacks and whatnot is just another part of the job."

Patrolmen Brus and Luzon, in fact, both cite the "security" of steady work and assured income as a prime advantage of being a New York City cop.

Both are white and live many miles from Harlem in mostly white middle-class suburbs. They're conservative family men for the most part, though rather long hair and sideburns reveal at least a mild desire to project a slightly more modish image.

Bob Brus is a stocky 34-year-old with piercing eyes and straight brown hair. His demeanor is serious, but he's relaxed—almost easygoing—most of the time. He speaks in a rather nasal, middle-class New York City accent.

Bob and his 31-year-old wife, Barbara, lived in the borough of Queens from childhood until five years ago. Then they bought a split-level, four-bedroom brick and frame house for $27,000 on a quiet, curving street in the Rockland County suburb of Orangetown, a 35-minute drive northwest of Harlem. Bob has added grass, shrubs and a permanent backyard swimming pool to the property, and he estimates the value of the home now at close to $50,000. The Bruses own two Buicks.

Though it would seem hard to finance all that on Bob's police salary of $11,500 a year, he says he manages by doing all his own yard work and his own house and auto repair. And Barbara points out that she worked as an executive secretary for a Manhattan wig company until she became pregnant with Bob Jr. "She made good money and essentially bought this house herself," says Bob, looking proudly out across his spacious backyard.

Bob hopes to quit the police force in four years if the police contract by then calls for retirement at half-pay after 15 years instead of the present 20, a change he believes is likely. At the moment, he's thinking of opening a franchised ice cream or hamburger drive-in after he leaves police work.

Jack Luzon, 25, has worked in Harlem a year and a half of his two and a half years on the force. He and his 23-year-old wife, Janet, and their son, Jack Jr., 4, live in a $155-a-month one-bedroom apartment in the Flushing section of Queens. Jack Sr. is slender with dark, wavy hair, and in voice, manner and appearance he slightly resembles Tony Curtis, the movie actor.

Jack drives a late-model Pontiac Le Mans with decals of the U.S. flag and the Playboy Bunny emblem on the back window. His current annual salary is $9,720, but Janet supplements that with her full-time job as a payroll bookkeeper at a Queens sunglass manufacturing company. The Luzons want to buy a house eventually, but "I just can't seem to save any money," Jack says.

The son of a retired police lieutenant, Jack says he became a cop mainly because "it looked more secure than baseball," one of his first loves. Jack played baseball throughout his youth, and had a tentative offer from the Baltimore Orioles a few years ago before he was drafted into the Army. He spends many off-duty hours in the summer now pitching for the police union's baseball team.

Janet Luzon worries considerably more about the dangers of Jack's job than he does. "I worry, and I have reason to," she says. "When I read about these attacks, I wonder to myself—it could be him, especially in that section of town. I wish he could have given baseball a little harder try."

Perhaps because she has confronted the problem longer, Barbara Brus isn't so concerned. "The danger's there; you sort of live with it. But if it worries you, you're going to be unhappy," she says. Sitting on a sofa in a black and white minidress in the Bruses' comfortable, tastefully furnished living room, Barbara says she doesn't feel Bob is in any more danger in Harlem than in areas with less crime. "These attacks are happening in the suburbs, too," she says.

That may be true. And, indeed, little happens to Bob Brus and Jack Luzon in a typical working day to indicate they are in any particular danger—though their on-the-job surroundings are forbidding enough.

Patrolmen Brus and Luzon work out of New York's 26th Precinct, which has its headquarters in a 90-year-old four-story converted warehouse on West 126th Street in Harlem. The decrepit dirty brick building is situated between the Disinfecting & Exterminating Corp. and the Old Homestead Bar in a block of four-story tenements and industrial buildings. The precinct includes densely populated Negro and Puerto Rican sections of West Harlem, but also the main campuses of Columbia University and the City University of New York and a strip of mainly white middle-class apartments along Riverside Drive west of Columbia near the Hudson River.

For Bob Brus and Jack Luzon, working together on the night shift, a fairly ordinary day's work goes like this:

4:03 p.m. The officers climb into a dark green, white and black police radio car, a slow-starting 1967 Plymouth four-door, where they will spend most of the next eight hours. Their radio call-sign is "Two Six Adam," designating the precinct and the section they're responsible for patrolling. The car is dirty inside and out and is dented in several places. On the floor of the back seat are a bent wire coat hanger, a scarred night stick, a piece of rope, an open match book and a few stale peanuts. A heavy steel mesh barrier separates the front and back seats, and the inside handles and locks are removed from the back doors so prisoners can't escape.

Both officers yawn a lot. Fatigue, in fact, is a constant problem for New York policemen, at least partly because they're required to change schedules every seven or eight days. For example, they work five days from 4 p.m. to midnight, then after 56 hours off switch to 8 a.m. to 4 p.m. The midnight-to-8 shift follows that. Because of the constant changes, the men seldom are as alert as they might be otherwise. "It keeps your stomach in an uproar," Officer Brus says.

4:20 p.m. Five teen-age Negro boys rush up to the patrol car at a corner in a tenement neighborhood. "There's a man over there waving a shotgun at us," yells one boy, pointing to a building around the corner. Patrolman Brus gets out of the car and saunters toward an elderly Negro man in faded blue coveralls and a green shirt sitting alongside the building. A dirty gray dog lounges at his feet. The officer chats with the man, then calls the boys together and confers with them.

"The shotgun turned out to be a golf club," Officer Brus says, getting back into the car. The old man is the superintendent of the building, and he told Patrolman Brus the boys were throwing bottles at the dog. He had tried to scare them out of the block with the golf club. "They have no place else to play, though," Bob says. "The park (half a block away) is full of dog leavings and they can't run around and tackle without stepping in it. So all you can do is tell 'em to quit bothering the dog and tell the old man to lay off the boys."

"Kids are sure different now," says Jack Luzon. "When I was a kid, even a teen-ager, we used to run when we saw a cop. We knew he'd whack us across the back of the legs with his night stick if we were hanging around a corner. If we went home and told our parents they'd say 'Good, you must have deserved it.' Now, these kids stand there and say 'Move? Why should I move?' And if you whack them, their parents come storming down to the precinct house hollering about police brutality."

4:38 p.m. The car cruises slowly east on 118th Street, a littered street of four- and five-story tenements. "Those two officers got shot last January right ahead there in the next block," Bob says. The wounded patrolmen, both of whom recovered, had responded to a phoned complaint of a "disorderly group" in the hallway of an apartment building, he recalls. It was about 11:30 at night. "They drove up, got out, and just as they stepped up on the curb, these guys opened up on them." Two men with guns were on a roof across the street, and another was in an open stairwell leading to an outside basement entrance of the building next door to the one the officers were approaching.

Such routine responses to calls for police aid are handled differently now in New York. "We don't get out of the car at the same time anymore. The recorder usually goes in first. If you're going to get shot, it's usually when you first get out of the car or right inside the front door," Bob Brus says. (The "recorder" is the officer who sits in the passenger seat and records the events of the day in a logbook. The driver and recorder normally trade places at the middle of their eight-hour shift.)

"They've also told the cars not all to converge at once in the street where the sniper is," Brus goes on. "Instead, some of us now are supposed to cover the surrounding streets. That way, if they're still shooting, they won't have as many cars to shoot at. And if they try to escape across the roofs, we have a chance of grabbing them."

Officers Brus and Luzon disagree on the reasons for the sniping attacks. "I personally think it's got to be an organized thing," Jack Luzon says. "We've seen Black Panther literature on how to kill cops, how to break down the government, how to do this, how to do that." But Bob Brus says: "I doubt if it's a conspiracy here; maybe it is in Philadelphia. I have a feeling it's just kooks here. The publicity helps keep these things going. Some kook probably reads about it and says to himself 'Well, they're shooting cops now. I think I'll go out and get me one, too.' "

4:45 p.m. "Two Six Adam," the police radio crackles, "respond to a disorderly person at four-one Morningside Avenue, Apartment One."

"Please ten-five (repeat) the address of that last job, central," Bob Brus replies. "There isn't any 41 Morningside. It's either got to be 40 or 50."

"Caller said 41," the dispatcher radios back. "Woman said she's going to be killed, by the way. We have no way of checking the address."

"Let's check 40," Bob says.

Officer Luzon makes a U-turn several blocks north and within a minute the car arrives at the address, a building that's maintained somewhat better than many in the area. The officers enter together and stand well to the side of the door to Apartment One as Bob Brus sounds the buzzer. There's no sound inside the apartment and no answer to a second buzz. The officers cross the hall and try the building superintendent's buzzer. He doesn't answer either. They shrug and return to the car.

Why did both officers leave the car and enter the building together when the new anti-sniper procedure calls for them to do so one at a time? For one thing, Bob says, Jack isn't his regular partner and they aren't used to working together. "Besides," he adds, "it's still daylight, and the shootings don't usually happen till after dark."

4:55 p.m. Bob Brus is out of the patrol car arranging for a recovered stolen car to be towed from a residential street near Riverside Drive. Jack Luzon is talking about the police baseball team: "The main reason we have the team is community relations. We play several Puerto Rican teams and a colored team, the Bronx Bombers. We get to know the other teams and they see that we're human—we have feelings, families and like baseball just like they do."

"Community relations is big nowadays, especially with the racial issue," he continues. "Working here was really hard for me at first. The colored people live differently, you know. I'd never seen any dope, gambling or prostitution growing up on the Island (Long Island). The laws are enforced differently here, too. We see dice games or drunks drinking out of a bottle in the street here and pass right on by. In Queens you don't see that sort of thing because the police break it up quick. Of course, there's more of it here. If we ran in every junkie or drunk we saw we'd do nothing else. And in this part of town when you make an arrest, you run the chance of having people gang up on you. They really stick together around here."

5:40 p.m. A middle-aged man, drunk or high on narcotics or both, staggers along 123d Street mumbling loudly but unintelligibly. "He's just letting off his frustrations," says Bob Brus with a chuckle as the police car drives past. The patrolmen frequently are in contact with addicts in connection with crimes junkies commit to support their habits. "The last one I locked up had a $160-a-day habit," Patrolman Brus says.

8:35 p.m. The officers leave the Campus Deli just west of Columbia after their evening meal. It's one of the first chilly evenings of the fading summer. Jack Luzon shivers in his short-sleeved light-blue uniform shirt and says, "The summer reruns are about over and the new fall TV shows will be starting. That should keep some of these troublemakers occupied for a while."

9:10 p.m. The two patrolmen have just given a sixtyish Negro man with a dead auto battery a ride to a service station when they're called to look for the prowler on the fire escape with the step missing near Columbia. They drop the man at his car, complete the prowler search and return to help the man start his car. The electric starter cable he borrows from the service station is faulty. "We paid Gulf $34.95 for that battery," moans the man's portly wife, waving a receipt. The officers take the man and the cable back to the service station, and he says he'll get another ride back to his car.

9:35 p.m. Car 26 Adam is sent to a well-kept three-story apartment building across the street from Columbia Law School. Two young French-speaking Negroes have allegedly just stolen $10 at knife point from Olga Mirosav, about 40, an employe at Columbia's foreign student center. Inside her second floor apartment, Miss Mirosav, a hefty woman in a gray sweater, slacks and shower clogs, nervously tells Officers Brus and Luzon the thieves were wearing sneakers and she hadn't heard them come up behind her at the front door of the building as she returned home from the beach. Patrolman

Luzon takes down the details, and the officers say they'll report the incident to the precinct's detective staff.

10:02 p.m. Prowlers are in the basement of another apartment building near Columbia, the radio says. Officers Luzon and Brus arrive at the scene at the same time as a second patrol car. The officers move in single file several yards apart down steps to a basement passageway. Fortunately the stairway is well lighted. The superintendent, who had called police, emerges from a cellar entrance to meet them. Suddenly and silently a tall black man and a young white man with long hair appear from around a corner in the passageway. Patrolman Luzon blinks and asks the superintendent: "Are these the ones?"

The superintendent looks sheepish. "Hell, they're the telephone men," he says. Everybody laughs. "I didn't know they were here, and I just didn't want to take any chances," the superintendent says.

10:17 p.m. Patrolman Luzon buys a corned beef sandwich at the West End Bar on Broadway and the officers take it to another policeman guarding a prisoner at a hospital several blocks away.

11:18 p.m. The police radio tells all cars that a policeman has been reported shot on 109th Street. "Probably a false alarm," mutters Patrolman Brus. A quick check with officers in the area proves him right. "You get a lot of these crank calls when the police are getting shot," he says.

11:32 p.m. "Dead night," Bob Brus says. "It's welfare check day, too; you'd have thought there'd be more action."

—DAVID MCCLINTICK

Animal Collector

DON Hunt brakes his Toyota Landcruiser beside a herd of Cape buffalo grazing on the slopes of Mount Kenya. He swings onto the kikuyu grass, a trim figure in a well-tailored, sleeveless safari suit. "Leave the door open," he says. "My friend Stupid might not be in a good mood."

"Stupid" is a big black bull with wicked-looking curved horns protruding from a bony mass atop his head. Hunters rate the Cape buffalo as one of the five most dangerous animals in Africa, along with the lion, the black rhinoceros, the elephant and the leopard. The Toyota seems slim protection against a 1,500-pound buffalo.

Cautiously, Don edges toward the beast. "I raised this animal from a calf, then set it free," he says over his shoulder. "But I've been in the Congo for awhile. It may have forgotten me."

Evidently it has. The animal glances at the man, lowers its head and stirs red dust with a hoof. It snorts. Then it turns and shuffles away.

Don Hunt returns, shaking his head. His job requires close contact with animals, and he isn't discouraged by one rebuff. He collects animals for zoos, research agencies and private collectors. His company, International Animal Exchange Inc., which he founded and heads as president, claims to be the biggest game collecting firm in the world.

"We supply 80% of the animals imported by American zoos," Don says as he slips behind the wheel of the Toyota. Ahead, a covey of Egyptian ibis are swooping over the white bulk of the swank Mount Kenya Safari Club, his operational headquarters. An eland bull, a variety of antelope, shuffles out of the Toyota's path. A Thompson's gazelle rises to its feet, tiny tail twitching semaphore signals of anxiety.

Pointing to a gully strewn with red rocks, Don recalls: "Last year, I caught six leopards at that spot. That wooded valley beyond is full of leopards."

Don Hunt is a ruddy-complexioned, wavy-haired Irishman from Detroit with a boyish grin and an evangelistic fervor where conservation and animal husbandry are concerned. At 39, he isn't yet ready to slide behind a desk, though his business has grown into a giant animal conglomerate that grossed about $6 million in 1970, double the volume of 1969. Three brothers provide the administrative talent from a Ferndale, Mich., base, while Don takes care of the more glamorous aspects of bringing them back alive from Africa.

A game collector, of course, collects lions, elephants, rhinos, leopards, cheetahs and anything else a client might want. Don's score includes five rare Somali wild asses for the Basel, Switzerland, zoo; over 200 cheetahs, an animal that faces extinction, plus all the more common animals. Now he is launching an expedition into the Ituri Forest of the Congo, aiming at the okapi, one of the world's rarest animals. The long-necked okapi looks like a cross between a giraffe and a chestnut-colored antelope, but is so shy that it is seldom seen by man.

Usually collectors concentrate on the babies or the young adults in an animal group. Despite wide publicity given to tranquilizer "bullets," Don believes much research still must be conducted before tranquilizers can be used without fear of injuring the animal. Meantime, he continues to use techniques he and other collectors have developed over the years.

Impala and Thompson's gazelle are hunted at night, using a powerful spotlight to blind the animals. As they stand hypnotized, the collector and his crew pounce on the ones they want. Lions and leopards are caught in traps, gorillas in hand-tossed nets when a family group is feeding on the ground.

"The best way to catch a cheetah is to grab it by the tail and toss it into a box," Don says. The collector might have to chase one of these animals in a "catcher car" first, since a cheetah can hit 60 miles an hour or more in short spurts.

An animal is never chased to exhaustion, though, Don warns. He has a well-developed time cycle for each animal. If the chase exceeds the allocated time, then the animal is allowed to run free. That time cycle, for instance, amounts to two minutes for a zebra, one and a half minutes for a giraffe, four minutes for a Somali ass, three minutes for an elephant and one and a half to three minutes for a cheetah. A stopwatch keeps tab of the time, from start of the chase to capture.

"If we exceed that time, there is too much danger that some internal organ may be injured, and the animal may die within six months," Don explains. The exertion may weaken a heart muscle or some other vital organ.

Sitting in the bar of the Safari Club, Don ticks off a list of delivered prices for animals. Among them: zebra, $2,000 to $2,500; giraffe, $5,000 to $6,500; small antelope, $1,000 to $4,000; rhinoceros, $7,000 to $10,000; leopard, $1,000 to $1,500; and lowland gorilla, $5,000 to $6,000.

What about highland gorilla? "I don't know," Don

says. "Nobody has caught one for the last 10 to 15 years." He himself plans, however, to try to catch some highland gorillas this year near Lake Kivu in the Congo.

One of the most expensive animals is the okapi, which brings $10,000 each. So many lions are being bred in zoos around the world that there is no market except for lions wanted for introducing new breeding stock into a pride. The price for such an animal is about $1,-500.

On the dusty plains east of Lake Rudolph in northern Kenya, Don and his crew demonstrate how the catcher car is used with plains animals. This is lava-strewn, semiarid country of vast spaces where isolated rocky buttes rise from the plains. The vegetation is mainly flat-topped acacias and patches of thorn bush. Game abounds, but the only other inhabitants are spear-toting Samburu tribesmen and their scrawny cattle.

Don's catcher car is a stripped-down Toyota that looks like a hot-rod racer. He climbs onto a platform just behind the driver, ready to maneuver a bamboo pole that juts from the side. A noose hangs from the end of the pole, with the other line tied to the vehicle.

Grevy's zebra are the quarry this day. Scores of these mule-like animals graze on a dry plain that seems to stretch endlessly to the Ethiopian border. Gears grinding, the catcher car rockets in pursuit. Don clings to a rollbar, which is a safeguard in case the car turns over. This is open country with no roads. Potholes are frequent and so are huge rocks. A zebra can run at close to 30 miles an hour, as startled animals demonstrate. The catcher car must hit 40 to 50 miles an hour to capture zebras, and up to 75 miles an hour when cheetah are the prey.

"We rolled over twice this year already," Don shouts cheerfully. "Fortunately, no one was hurt."

The catcher car accelerates, rocking and bumping behind a dozen running zebras. Dust rolls from hoofs. The animals show terror in every movement. The catcher car almost nudges the rump of one straining zebra. The vehicle swerves. Don grabs for a tighter hold as his feet leave the floor, then come down hard.

The car's driver brings the vehicle abreast of a young zebra with flying mane and fear-crazed eyes. Don maneuvers the bamboo pole over the animal's head. The noose drops and tightens. The driver slows the car and stops. The zebra bucks like a bronco at the end of the rope.

Don leaps to the ground with two African assistants. One grabs the zebra's head, the other its tail. Don loosens the noose to avoid injuring the animal.

A following truck jerks to a dust-raising stop. More Africans join the melee, grabbing for legs of the animal. A box-like paddock is unloaded from the truck and moved toward the animal. Everybody pushes the zebra into this container. A door slams. With a heave, men lift the box onto the back of the truck. In minutes the captured zebra is on its way to the "acclimatization" corral.

"Catching an animal is the easy part," Don says. "It's after capture that the work starts."

Every wild animal must undergo an adaptation period. Diet must be changed. In the wild, animals such as elephants, rhinos, giraffes and antelope live on local vegetation, of course. In zoos, they will be fed a mixture of oats, corn and soybeans. But it takes slow training to revise diets.

Animals must become accustomed to man, too, and they must adjust to the shock of losing their freedom.

In the case of a zebra, this takes a minimum of six weeks.

Standing beside a corral containing eight Grevy's zebra, Don explains that for the first few days of captivity, his aides will spend 10 hours a day talking to the zebras. Sometimes tapes of traffic, jet plane and ship noises are played in corrals to accustom animals to the sounds of civilization and of the long trips to distant zoos.

Before shipment, there's a 60-day quarantine in Mombasa and another 30 days at Clifton, N.J., for animals going to the U.S. Most animals up to the size of a rhino travel by air. Bigger animals go by ship.

"We spend $500,000 a year on air freight," Don says.

Among the orders Don has filled in the past 12 months were a cheetah for the Brookfield, Ill., zoo, another cheetah for the Cleveland zoo, a giraffe for the Detroit zoo, some Thompson's gazelles for the Oklahoma City zoo, a rhinoceros for the Toledo zoo and one for the Cincinnati zoo. A new zoo at Brownsville, Texas, is taking some $1.5 million of animals, half of which already have been delivered.

"There is no single most dangerous animal," Don says. "It depends on the place and the situation. Even an innocent-looking Thompson's gazelle can be dangerous in certain situations."

A gorilla once gave Don a particularly close call in Cameroon in west Africa. A family group of gorillas had been surrounded in bush country with the aid of Pygmy helpers and a pack of dogs. The big gorillas took to the trees, leaving youngsters to fend for themselves. One was captured.

But one of the dogs set up a howl in the brush, and, thinking the dog was hurt, Don shoved toward it. "I saw the dog first," he recalls. "Then I glanced down and saw the biggest foot I ever saw in my life. It seemed to be a yard long."

A full-grown male gorilla sat on the ground, half concealed by a bush. At sight of Don, it lunged forward, swinging a huge fist. The overhand right caught Don on the side of the head, knocking him out. "I spent the next 10 days in the hospital, thinking how wonderful it was that the gorilla had swung at me instead of grabbing me," he says. "A gorilla can crush a man with one squeeze, you know."

Another time, in the front yard of his home here, Don was charged by a "tame" eland. It tossed him about 20 feet through the air. Then it bent forward, its 30-inch long spiraled horns poised like two spears to drive through him. Don rolled over and evaded the horns. On all fours, he scrambled for his front door, making it just ahead of the animal. "The eland had a sore eye, and I wanted to look at it. I should have known better than try that without first immobilizing the animal," he says.

Don tries to remain apolitical as he plies his trade in African nationalist nations. He says that most of these nations now are conscious of the value of conservation, and he spends a lot of time nowadays assisting various game departments in conservation tasks.

In Kenya, he has been collecting zebra for the game department. Much of his time in the first half of 1971 will be spent in the Congo. President Mobutu of that country has invited him to reestablish the Epulu Okapi Station, which was destroyed during the Congo rebellion. This station, a unique facility in the Ituri Forest, was the only okapi reserve in the world. Don is also slated to establish a new game farm in the Lake Kivu area of the eastern Congo.

Then he will go to Ethiopia, where the game department has asked him to collect some rare hartebeest, which face extinction if left to face poachers in the Rift Valley. Ethiopia wants the animals captured and transported to a game park established on the Awash River near Gelila.

"The more I know about animals, the more I like and respect them," Don says. More than once he has become so attached to a particular animal that he has kept it for a pet or freed it in a game reserve.

A year-and-a-half-old leopard paces back and forth in a wire enclosure of "The Orphanage," a place for homeless animals that Don has established here. Don shakes his head no when asked if he will sell the animal for its $1,000 to $1,500 value.

"This one is part of the family," he says. He calls to the leopard, thrusts a hand through the fence and fondles the animal's nose. "A hunter killed this leopard's mother. It was such a cute cub, I kept it and raised it here at the orphanage. When it is big enough to fend for itself, I'll take it to a game reserve and set it free."

Twitch, a full grown cheetah, follows Don like a playful kitten. Stupid, the Cape buffalo, had been bottle fed by Don when the animal was orphaned as a calf. Their comradeship reached the point where Don could ride the buffalo as if it were a pony. But the star of the animal household is Jon-Jon, a six-year-old chimpanzee caught in the Congo. Jon-Jon frequently accompanies Don on safaris.

Don grew up in the animal business. At 11, he couldn't quite swing the purchase of a springer spaniel pup with his newsboy savings, so he went to work in a pet shop in Detroit. This after-school job continued through high school and three years at the University of Detroit. After a two-year hitch in the Army, he returned to Detroit to buy the shop. A big guinea pig order from Parke-Davis & Co., the drug maker, propelled him into the wholesale animal business. Soon he was importing animals from around the world

In the late 1950s one chimpanzee that arrived in Don's shop proved so appealing that he kept it and trained it. A friend at a Detroit television station helped launch Don as a TV performer known as "Bwana Don," with his chimpanzee friend Bongo Bailey. "It wasn't an African program," Don says. "It was set in fantasy-land for children."

The program was popular enough to be packaged in a series of 130 shows. "Six months of filming work was worth about $150,000 for me. I had the capital to start the International Animal Exchange," Don says.

That company now has grown into a diverse and profitable outfit. It operates three "Bwana Don" pet shops in Detroit and is launching a chain of franchised pet shops around the United States. It operates the African Safari Game Park in Port Clinton, Ohio, and last September opened the $2 million World of Animals Game Park near Dallas. Don plans to open a string of similar game parks in places as far removed as West Germany and Hawaii.

In the World of Animals parks, in which International Animal Exchange has a 25% interest and which it is hired to manage, 1,500 animals representing more than a score of species roam through nine compounds covering 550 acres. People drive through in automobiles while lions, baboons, giraffes and zebras wander through countryside landscaped in African style. The compounds are arranged so that natural enemies are separated.

"We are convinced we will prove to the zoos that the only way to handle animals is in an open park style," Don says. "In 10 years' time there will be zoos like this around the world."

Don says the idea of caging people in autos while the animals roam free came from Jimmy Chipperfield, a British circus man. Today there are five such parks in Britain, operated by different groups.

Don says wildlife is disappearing so fast in Africa that one day the continent may have to turn to zoos and game parks in America and elsewhere for animals that once were native to that continent. An interest in conserving the remaining species led him, he says, to launch the Mount Kenya Game Ranch a few years ago along with actor William Holden, Los Angeles attorney Deane Johnson and Julian McKeand, a Kenya game warden.

On 1,216 acres of open mountain slope and forest country near here, they have assembled 200 animals of 30 different species.

Though he was known as Bwana Don back in his television days in the late '50s, it wasn't until 1961 that Don made his first trip to east Africa. He liked it so much that he has gone back to the States only on brief business trips. He is separated from his wife, who lives in Michigan with their four children.

Don resides in a comfortable $25,000 house in Kenya. Sweeping a hand to encompass the view of the countryside from his wide front window, he says: "This is my home, and this is where I want to stay."

—RAY VICKER

Hurricane Hunters

THE Air Force reconnaissance plane enters the wall of turbulence ringing the eye of Hurricane Laurie, and dozens of wires, pipes and cables running along the plane's spine vibrate like cello strings. Life preservers hanging in the cabin swing in wide, erratic arcs, and eight stomachs heave through a half-hour roller coaster ride that sends everything not bolted down into the air.

Thin roast beef sandwiches, pencils and apples, milk containers, peanuts, navigation charts, chewing gum and plastic spoons are tossed into an aeronautical salad every time the plane drops 20 feet or so and pitches sideways. And this is only "moderate" turbulence, the crew assures a hitching reporter.

The crew of the four-engine, prop-jet WC-130B Hercules transport of the Air Force's 53rd Weather Reconnaissance Squadron takes the pitching and yawing in stride. Flying into eyes of hurricanes is their job, and though they have been criticized for not sending their warnings soon enough most people agree they have saved hundreds of lives by plotting the courses of hurricanes and warning when and where they will strike.

The military has been flying into hurricanes on purpose since World War II, and the work is likely to continue even though satellites now are used for much weather forecasting. Satellites can take pictures of whole hurricanes to chart their movement, but they can't measure the forces inside the storms, which indicate their severity. It's unlikely such a probing satellite will be developed in the near future, experts say.

"I really don't believe that there will be any development in any area within the next five to 10 years that will eliminate the need for aerial reconnaissance," says Arnold L. Sugg, deputy director of the National Hurricane Center in Miami. The national center orders and coordinates Air Force and Navy hurricane penetration and issues warnings about such storms. The Navy hurricane probers fly out of Jacksonville, Fla.; the Air Force team flies out of Puerto Rico.

The 1969 hurricane-spotting season, which lasted from June 1 to Nov. 1, was especially tough. Deadly Camille proved to be "the greatest storm of any kind that ever affected this nation," according to a man at the National Hurricane Center. Debbie was particularly hazardous to fly through because of severe icing on the planes. Inga, possibly the longest-lived hurricane in history, had to be tracked and penetrated for a month. And Laurie, another long-lasting storm, caused trouble by changing its course often. In all, the Navy and Air Force made hundreds of hurricane flights during the season.

No two flights are alike, but the flight into Laurie is fairly typical, according to crew members. The plane takes off on an overcast, October day from Ramey Air Force Base in Puerto Rico, stops to refuel at a base near Tampa and then heads for Laurie. Out of Tampa, the trip is smooth for about an hour. Then, after the half hour of turbulence, Capt. Marvin A. Lillie, a veteran of Camille, flies the Hercules into the calm of the eye. The sun is shining, and the slate-blue thunderclouds nearby are reflected in the unrippled sea below.

It is sometimes difficult to find the precise center of the eye, the spot where the temperature is highest, the pressure lowest and the sea calmest. It is here that a seven-pound measuring device called a dropsonde is parachuted out of the plane to radio back its findings to the hurricane center in Miami. These devices are dropped every two to four hours to enable trackers to chart the storm. Determining the center of Laurie's 35-mile-wide eye proves to be difficult, as evidenced by radio chatter between Capt. Lillie and his crew.

"This has got to be it."

"You want to check it out?"

(Pause.)

"I think we missed it."

"This is the strangest one I've seen in a long time."

"There's no white caps now; hardly a swell."

"My temperature's up pretty high."

"Below me, it's just like a mirror. I think this is it, fellas. Let's get straight and level."

(Pause.)

"No, we've passed the goddam thing again."

Capt. Lillie banks the Hercules steeply, maintaining its 10,700-foot altitude, and doubles back. Capt. Frederick J. Foss, the plane's weather officer, meanwhile checks the outside atmospheric pressure and air temperature. The plane eventually finds the center of the eye, and ejects the dropsonde.

At this point, the hurricane is spinning 250 miles west of Ft. Myers, Fla., and no one knows whether it will strike the Gulf Coast, dissipate or move back south where it came from. It already has looped once—very unusual for a Gulf hurricane—and has stayed in the Gulf of Mexico longer than any hurricane the men in the Hercules can remember. Its 75-mile-an-hour winds barely put it in the hurricane category but that, too, could change suddenly.

Nearly everything about a hurricane can change suddenly. The eye of Laurie, for instance, has changed dramatically, in the three hours before Capt. Lillie piloted his Hercules into her. Says Capt. Foss: "Three hours ago another plane from the squadron penetrated, and they found the eye very clearly defined. They also found a hell of a lot of turbulence, and they took a pretty good pounding." During those three hours, he speculates, Laurie bounced off a cold front, which apparently split the storm in half and weakened it.

The elusive eye makes Laurie all the tougher to track. "Camille was well-defined," says Capt. Foss. "It was easy to locate, not very turbulent, and getting in and out was generally smooth. Now, this is a tough hurricane. It's badly defined, and seems to be breaking up, which makes it very hard to measure."

Flying into a hurricane isn't as hazardous as it seems, the crew says reassuringly. Hurricanes have strong sides and weak sides, and the procedure is to fly through the weak side into the eye. Spiraling rain clouds, called feeder bands, radiate out from the eye like the tentacles of an octopus that is spinning counterclockwise. So, to make the flying even easier, the pilots try to slip between the feeder bands on the weak side. It's generally too dangerous to try to fly over the storm's walls, pilots say.

"It's really not that dangerous if you do it the right way," says Capt. Foss. "And we do it the right way."

Indeed, there have been few casualties among hurricane hunters. The 53rd Squadron has never lost a plane, though a sister squadron that hunts typhoons out of Guam lost two planes and their nine-man crews in the 1950s. A Navy squadron lost a plane in Hurricane Janet in 1955. Generally, says Capt. Foss, what danger there is comes mainly from icing on the wings and engines. Even so, he adds, "I'd prefer to have flown through Camille than to have been on the ground and in its path."

Camille, which struck in mid-August of 1969, left 259 persons dead and 68 missing in Mississippi, Louisiana, Alabama, Virginia and West Virginia. It also caused millions of dollars in damages from water and winds, which reached 200 miles an hour.

As Capt. Lillie is discussing how relatively safe it is to fly into a hurricane, he lets out with a loud curse. The generator in one of the plane's right engines has stopped. He turns off the engine, and announces the plane will head for Homestead Air Force Base near Miami rather than going back to Puerto Rico. He assures everyone there is no danger.

But then he starts talking about engine failure, and the crew starts telling the reporter their favorite "war stories" about engines conking out. "Icing was very bad in Debbie," says Capt. Gary W. Gates, the copilot. "We penetrated Debbie at 10,000 feet, got data and our fixes, and decided to save fuel by flying out over the top, instead of through it. We tried to climb to 25,000 feet, but at 22,000 we started picking up heavy icing. The number four engine started to flame out (stop) at 24,500, and ice built up so fast you couldn't see out of the window. We got out of the ice before the engine actually died, but it would have flamed out in another 30 seconds."

And he adds not so reassuringly: "Under those circumstances, we couldn't have stayed in the air—if that engine died, I mean." But Capt. Lillie repeats that his three-engine plane is in no danger, and indeed before long he lands it perfectly at Homestead. There, the generator is taken out, to eliminate the risk of fire, and then the plane takes off for its home base in Puerto Rico, where it lands barely 10 hours after taking off from there in search of Laurie. (The generators in the other three engines provide enough electricity to run the fourth engine.)

When Capt. Gates flew into Debbie, he was trying to break up the storm by dropping silver iodide particles into its eye. The experiment, known as Project Stormfury, didn't appear to affect Debbie one way or another. She died a natural death at sea several days later.

Laurie also died at sea, much to the relief of the Hurricane Center people, who for a while thought she would strike the U.S. with ferocity. Warnings had been issued to residents of the Gulf states that a hurricane was on its way.

The hurricane fighters and the hurricane center think they serve their purpose if they can sound their warnings at least 12 daylight hours before a storm strikes. Not everyone thinks that that is enough time, however. Some Washington officials, for instance, think the South was not given enough warning about Camille, though it got more than a 12-hour notice.

There are other complaints about the hurricane-fighting operation. After touring the devastation left by Camille, Vice President Spiro Agnew said that the government has found that the Navy has excellent meteorological equipment on its planes but that the planes themselves are not up to the pounding they must take. The Air Force planes, on the other hand, can take the punishment but lack the most modern equipment, he said. The matter now is being studied in Washington.

There is truth in what the Vice President said. Most of the specialized equipment in the WC-130B that flew into Laurie is designed for air sampling, rather than for collecting storm data, but the plane is reputedly one of the most overpowered in the Air Force. The Navy planes —propeller-driven WC121 Constellations—were designed for airline use. They tend to handle clumsily in very bad weather but are loaded with electronic equipment, including powerful radar.

Air Force and Navy hurricane hunters can at least find consolation in their planes' interior appointments, which, while hardly luxurious, are made as safe as possible. That includes padded ceilings in their cockpits.

"Once, we had a weather officer bounced off the ceiling," says a pilot in the 53rd, "and it didn't even give him a headache."

— WILLIAM E. BURROWS

A Top Connector

THREE hundred feet above a downtown Chicago street, Tom West straddles a beam on the uppermost edge of a new skyscraper. A derrick lifts a long piece of I-shaped steel to him. He grabs an end of it, grapples it into place on an upright column and slips a bolt through the matching holes on the two members. Then he gets to his feet and unconcernedly walks out on the eight-inch-wide beam to remove the wire noose by which it hung from the derrick. This accomplished, he plunks himself down on the naked steel to await the next piece.

For that sort of aerial derring-do, Tom West earns $8.60 an hour plus assorted fringe benefits. When the weather permits, and it often doesn't on winter days, he works 40 hours a week. Last year his pay came to about $11,000.

The thought of falling and being killed has occurred to him. In his 12 years as an ironworker, the stocky, affable 38-year-old has seen several fellow workmen plunge to their deaths, and he has had a few close calls himself. Still, he doesn't dwell on that sort of thing. "I always think that the other guy will get it, not me," he says with a shrug.

In all, he's happy with his job. "The money is pretty good, I'm out in the air and I like the guys I work with," he says. Besides, he laughs, "I like being able to do something that scares the hell out of other people."

To most other people, of course, even the idea of doing the kind of work Tom does is enough to cause shivers, and well it should. Despite advances in construction safety over the past few years, the on-the-job fatality rate among ironworkers, who put up the steel skeletons of buildings and bridges, is the highest of any sizable job category in the U.S. According to the National Safety Council, 1.29 ironworkers died for each million man-hours worked in the trade from 1967 through 1969. This was more than twice the rate for underground coal miners, the next most dangerous occupation.

Tom's union, the International Association of Bridge, Structural and Ornamental Iron Workers, says that more than 500 of its members have lost their lives in job-connected accidents in the past five years.

For the average sidewalk superintendent, however, a more compelling consideration might be acrophobia, the fear of heights that seizes many persons when they as much as lean out a second-story balcony. Dr. Leonard Elkun, a psychiatrist in the University of Chicago School of Medicine, says that this reaction has little to do with any real fear of falling. "What happens is that for a split second your realize how easy it would be to lose control and end it all by jumping," he says. "The impulse is quickly countered—you reassure yourself that your feet are firmly planted and you're not going to do it—but it lasts long enough to cause a slightly turned stomach or a tingle in the spine."

Dr. Elkun continues that a mild form of acrophobia is "ubiquitous . . . maybe 95 of 100 people have it." Men who can work daily in high, exposed places "are decidedly unaverage in that respect and probably others," he says.

Of the 175,000 or so men in this trade, Tom West belongs to the group that goes the highest of all. Like most journeymen ironworkers, he can do any job on a steel erection site, but he usually works as a "connector." These are the men who first climb the beams and columns to temporarily link new steel into place with single, hand-tightened bolts. Then other ironworkers take over, aligning the new steel with tight wire cables and permanently bolting and welding it.

It's only after the ironworkers finish their jobs that the cement masons, electricians, pipe fitters, carpenters, elevator installers and the numerous other tradesmen involved in a high-rise building can do theirs.

Being "first up" is one of the things that gives ironworkers an unusually strong pride of craft. This sentiment is expressed in a number of ways, the most obvious being their continuing attachment to the term "ironworker" even though buildings and bridges have been built with steel, not iron, for decades. The label is retained because it helps set the bearers apart from steelworkers, whom they see as having tame, indoor jobs.

Ironworkers' on-the-job terminology is a good deal more blunt, to say the least; an apprentice is a "punk," and a foreman is a "pusher." What's more, ironworker foremen are union members and the line between them and the men they direct is thin. Most veteran ironworkers, including Tom West, have been "pushers" themselves on one project or another.

Finally, if an ironworker doesn't cut the mustard on a job he can be summarily ordered off of it by the contractor, usually without complaint from the union. This is a rare practice in American labor, but it is supported by the men in the craft. That's because no ironworker wants to risk working with someone who is incompetent. An ironworker with a bad job record soon comes to be known (for reasons lost in history) as a "Joe McGee." He sometimes has other distinguishing features. "You can tell the Joes by their (mangled) fingers and toes," goes the saying in the trade.

On top of all this, ironworkers have an internal hierarchy based on the danger of their tasks, with connectors like Tom West on the top of it. "To listen to ironworkers talking in a bar, you'd think that every one of them is, was or is going to be a top connector," smiles Bob Tipton, a lean, tobacco-chewing Tennessean who spent more than a dozen years as a connector and now is steel erection superintendent on Tom's current job, an office building that will rise 35 stories above the Chicago River on the western edge of this city's "Loop."

Actually, only about one ironworker in 10 on a high-rise project works as a connector, and Bob Tipton says that not all of them do the job the way it should be done.

"You can tell a good man by the way he handles himself on the iron—how he stations himself and how he moves," says the 43-year-old superintendent. "A man's got to be strong, but he's also got to have common sense. When the metal comes up, he can't be on the Arkansas (wrong) side. He's got to be set so he can swing the piece the way it ought to go. If he can't swing the piece right, that piece will swing him."

You can also tell a "top" connector by the way other ironworkers treat him, Bob Tipton says. "He's always got a place to hang his coat."

Tom West is regarded as a first-rate connector even though he is untypical of the breed in some respects. For one thing, at age 38 he is several years past the point when most connectors have stepped down permanently to "pushing," welding or other less arduous tasks. For another, at a roundish 5-feet, 9-inches tall and 175 pounds, he doesn't fit the rangy mold of his specialty.

But his appearance is deceiving. "Every time I come on a new job the superintendent looks at this gut of mine and thinks 'What the hell is this guy doing here?' " he says. "But when he sees me climbing around for a day or two, he knows I'm okay."

Tom West was born and raised in Oglesby, Ill., a town of some 4,000 residents about 100 miles west of Chicago. He was one of a family of seven brothers and four sisters. He says he "wasn't any good" at school and his family was poor, so when he graduated from grammar school at 15 he added a year to his age and went to work with his father in a local cement mill.

Tom got his start doing high work several years later as a moonlighter, putting up the 50-foot antenna towers that people around his hometown needed to get television programs from Chicago. He found that heights didn't bother him, so he progressed to bigger jobs.

"We were on strike once, and a fellow asked me to put up a 250-foot smokestack on his factory. I'd never been up that high, and I wasn't sure I could, but I told him I'd try. He had another guy there for a day to show me how to do it, and then he let me alone. I put the whole thing together myself. Man, it was great up there. I loved it."

The money was all right, too, Tom says; he was earning $2.50 an hour on his moonlighting jobs, compared with just $1.85 an hour as a cement mill maintenance man.

Still, Tom stayed at the mill for 11 years; it was only after it closed in 1958 that he took to ironworking full time. Instead of going through the Iron Workers' union apprenticeship program, he began by doing "permit work," which union locals dispense to nonmembers when there is more demand for workmen than they can supply. After three years of collecting "permit slips" certifying satisfactory job performance, he obtained his union "book"—journeyman's card—from a local in Canada that didn't have an apprenticeship program. In return, Tom continues to pay dues of $10 a month to that local, though he never has worked in Canada. He also pays dues and assessments to the Iron Workers' local in the area where he works.

For most of his years in the craft, Tom has "boomed around" from job to job the way most ironworkers do. He has helped put up a steel mill in central Illinois, a missile-control center in North Dakota, a nuclear power plant in Iowa, skyscrapers in Chicago and highway bridges all over the Midwest. Mostly, the work has been steady and the pay good. His best years were 1967 and 1968, when he made about $16,000 annually working almost exclusively on a giant steel mill for Jones & Laughlin Steel Corp. in Hennepin, Ill. That job required considerable overtime.

In 1969 and 1970, Tom's pay dropped to about $11,000 a year. Both years he took two-month vacations, spending most of the time working on two small apartment buildings he purchased in Oglesby. He makes his home in one of the buildings with Julianne, his 27-year-old wife, and one of his four children by a previous marriage, which ended in divorce. When he works in Chicago, he lives in a suburb with a brother, an official of a suburban bank, and commutes to Oglesby on weekends.

Tom says he could have made more money the past two years if he had foregone his vacations and been willing to take jobs farther from home. "But I've had enough of that for a while," he says. "My wife's got a terrific disposition, and she keeps a great house, and I really appreciate that. I had enough of chasing around the country for those couple of years I was single."

For his wife's part, she wishes Tom were home more, but she says she's "not complaining." She adds: "He's doing what he likes, and that's okay with me."

Tom has suffered his share of bumps and bruises at work, but he has never been seriously injured, a fact he ascribes mostly to luck. He says the worst thing that ever happened to him on a job was when a welder accidentally spilled some molten metal down his shirt collar. "Ooooo, that smarted. I had a couple blisters you wouldn't have believed," he recalls.

He continues, however, that he has come close to disaster on several occasions. "A bunch of times I've slipped off the iron and had to hold on," he says. "Once, on the ground, I got whacked in the head with a swinging piece of steel and got knocked cold. Another time, I was working with a torch about 90 feet off the ground, dismantling a big enclosed conveyor at a factory. A piece of the darned thing broke off while I was standing in it. It looked like a big funnel tilting down. If I hadn't grabbed the handle of a hopper car standing on a solid part, I would have gone down with it."

He has seen much worse. At the new McCormick Place Convention Center in Chicago, he watched as a crane section tipped over, skidded down rows of arena seats and struck a workman, killing him. "It knocked him a block," says Tom, shaking his head.

Before that, at Hennepin, "a roofer tripped or something and fell 60 feet to a cement floor. I was on a rafter below and he went past me so close I could have touched him." That man died, too.

"The unforeseen is what gets you," Tom muses. "Guys never get hurt when they're just walking on beams, no matter how dangerous it looks. It's when something slips and drops or breaks. That's why there's no use worrying about it. When it happens, there's nothing you can do."

Ironworkers go highest on skyscraper buildings, but perhaps surprisingly they consider that sort of work among the least hazardous that they do. That's because most high-rises are erected in tiers of two stories each with temporary floors on each tier, so workmen are never more than 25 feet or so above a floor. They can fall over the side of the building, of course, but those in the industry say this rarely happens.

A high-rise is built atop caissons that are made of steel-reinforced concrete and extend down to bedrock. Steel columns, weighing as much as 15 tons each on the bottom floors, begin to rise vertically from the caissons in sections of about 25 feet. At each story, horizontal beams connect the columns and lighter pieces of steel connect the beams. Wood planking is laid on every other floor, the derrick that hoists materials to the work area is taken apart and lifted, and the process is repeated until the structure is completed.

Every piece of steel is specially fabricated and numbered before it reaches the building site. It all fits together according to plan.

Engineers say that by working in this manner, an edifice of almost any height can be put up. "The reasons we don't build 300-story buildings are psychological and economic, not structural," says an official of U.S. Steel Corp.'s American Bridge division, which fabricates the steel and erects the framework of numerous bridges and buildings.

Safety precautions abound on the building site. Every ironworker on an American Bridge project is given a 64-page booklet of safety dos and don'ts. He is issued a reinforced plastic hardhat, tinted goggles and a wide leather belt on which to hang his tools. Each belt also holds a length of nylon rope that the ironworker is supposed to tie to something solid when he is working in an exposed place for any length of time.

The men furnish their own nonslip boots and avoid wearing loose or torn clothing. Their cold-weather outfits consist of thermal underwear, at least two pairs of socks, several layers of shirts and sweatshirts and a heavy jacket or quilted coveralls. To this, some of them add safety wrinkles of their own. Tom, for instance, wears heelless shoes that won't catch when he walks on the beams.

Teams of riveters slinging and driving hot rivets used to be a colorful part of the ironworking trade, but rivets have almost entirely been replaced by high-strength bolts during the past decade. The impetus for this move was mainly economic—two bolters can do the work that used to require a highly skilled four-man riveting team—but the elimination of the riveter's forge and the practice of tossing and catching the red-hot fasteners has added measurably to building safety, construction men say.

In addition, ironworkers don't work when it's too cold (anywhere near zero), too windy (gusts up to 25 miles an hour) or rainy. Some say that rain makes the steel too slippery to handle, but others suspect that ironworkers just don't like to get wet. "If one drop hits you, that's the Lord's fault; if two drops hit you, that's your fault," says Bob Tipton.

Safety, however, doesn't always come first. For example, every ironworker knows that the safest way to move horizontally on exposed steelwork is by "cooning," a process that involves putting one foot on each side of the bottom flange of an "I" beam, one hand on each side on the top flange, and then scurrying along on all fours, like a raccoon. But "cooning" is deemed proper only in especially hazardous situations, such as in traversing a beam that's still hanging from a derrick wire. "To be a real ironworker, you've got to get off your ass and onto your feet," says Tom.

It isn't enough to just walk on the steel; to be esteemed by his colleagues, an ironworker must do it with a businesslike clump, his hands swinging normally at his sides instead of stretched out tightrope-walker style.

On top of all this, connectors like Tom West eschew such niceties as ladders in moving up and down the levels of steelwork on a structure. When going down, they wrap their arms and legs around a column and slide, the way a fireman goes down a pole. Going the other way, they grab the near flange of a column with their hands, put their feet on the far flange and walk right up. It's safer to take a ladder, "but I sure look a lot better doing it the other way," says Tom.

Most serious accidents stem from falls, but there are numerous other dangers. These were apparent when Tom was connecting steel on what will be the 24th floor of his current job. It was cool, with the temperature in the high 30s, and a light but sometimes gusty wind was sweeping the top level of planking from which about 50 men worked. A haze limited vision, but several miles of Chicago's low, gray and brown West Side stretched below in one direction and the taller buildings of the Loop loomed on another. The view straight down from the sideless platform was clear; the Chicago River wound green and narrow, and the noontime streets swarmed.

The work floor was cluttered with tools, sections of steel and the cables that drive the air or electric-powered machines the men use. Power bolting tools set up a raucous clatter. Welders' torches blazed, sending sprays of sparks down to the floors below. The most frequent though least serious type of injury in steel erection is the eye burns that occur when a workman looks directly into a welder's flash, so the men avert their eyes. Thousand-pound beams swung from two derricks whose masts towered 115 feet above the planking.

Two connecting crews of seven men each were at work putting up new steel, one on each derrick. A crew consists of a foreman, two connectors, two men who load steel onto the derrick cable from the work floor, a man who operates the derrick's mast and boom and a man with a telephone headset who directs the hoist operator on the ground in lifting and lowering loads. The hoist operator goes solely by the phone man's instructions; he can't see what's happening on the floors above. The cables that do the lifting go up the center of the building, through the mast and out the boom.

It's a delicate team operation. Tom's connecting partner is Bob Beall, a lanky man of 27 who sports steel-rimmed glasses, a drooping mustache and hair that hangs over his collar. Bob spends his summers in Colorado as a mountain-climbing guide, an avocation that his fellow ironworkers find amusing. "Bob's half-hippie and a little nuts, but he's okay," says Tom, whacking his partner in the ribs with an elbow.

The boom and hoist operators and the phone man do their jobs well, accurately swinging the rust-orange steel up to Tom and Bob, but not without frequently banging the beams on existing steel on the way up. When that happens, men on the work floor are showered with rust particles and the upper levels of the steelwork shake noticeably.

The steel fits together better on the blueprints than it does on the job, so the two connectors have to manhandle many pieces into place, often kicking and jumping on them. For particularly difficult connections, a crowbar-like tool is brought into play. It is hot work, even in the cool air, and both men soon are sweating heavily.

There hadn't been a lost-time accident on the job since it was started, and there wasn't any on this day. Once, a swinging piece of steel banged into a column only inches above Tom's hand, but he later said he knew where it was all the time. One of the loaders was struck on the back by an errant derrick hook, but he merely rubbed the injured spot and kept working.

After work, relaxing over a beer, Tom allows that he won't be able to continue ironworking forever. He says that when he can't be a connector any longer, he'll quit the trade. He admits that he isn't as agile as he used to be. "At one time I could do somersaults on the iron—I really could," he says.

He says that his banker brother owns a piece of land across from a high school in Lombard, Ill., the suburb where he lives, and is thinking of opening a hamburger restaurant on it. Tom says that an existing restaurant a few blocks from the school is "a gold mine," and he's sure that a closer one would do even better. If it's built, he'll probably operate it, he says.

But he adds that he's in no hurry to quit ironworking. "It gets in your blood, you know," he says. "I had a motorcycle once, and that was the way it was with it, too. I could just keep going up and down those hills all day. I never wanted to turn around and go home."

—Frederick C. Klein

The Old Pro

VINCE Costello, middle linebacker for the pro football New York Giants, made a concession to age at the team's training camp at Fairfield University in Connecticut the summer he was 36 years old. He bought an air-conditioner for his dormitory room.

"I used to be able to move around in the heat all day and not feel it too much, but I can't any more," Vince said one hot July day as he gratefully plopped his 6-foot, 230-pound frame on a bed in the cool room after a 90-minute practice session. "The first few days at camp are always the worst. If I can make it through the first week, it's downhill the rest of the way."

Not surprisingly, Costello made it through that first week and through the rest of the two-month training session; 11 previous seasons in the National Football League had made him an expert in survival.

Vince Costello is not a $100,000-a-year superstar. His name isn't in the sports headlines or the society or fashion pages. He has never been an all-pro. The only products he has ever been asked to endorse are ball bearings. He is not the idol of millions of little boys and big girls.

For Vince Costello, football is simply a job. And while he says it is still an enjoyable occupation, it is one fraught with hazards and uncertainties never faced by practitioners of most other trades. Right now, for instance, Costello's career is nearing an end, at an age when others of the same educational level—he has a master's degree in guidance counseling—are just beginning to rise.

"I've considered retiring every winter after the last five seasons, but I know that when I quit my income immediately will be cut in half," says Vince, who earns something more than $30,000 a year for his football efforts and gets several thousand more from outside investments. "I'll keep going as long as I think I can physically, and as long as my team has a shot at a good season."

In pro football, however, retirement isn't always voluntary. When a pro player's performance no longer measures up, he is unceremoniously cut by his team and left to his own devices.

Players not only are dropped at will but also are bought and sold like sides of beef. After 10 years with the Cleveland Browns, Costello was traded to the Giants in 1967. He naturally had no say in the transaction, though he likes being a Giant. "At Cleveland, they got so used to seeing me around they convinced themselves I was too old," he says. But in New York, the Giants "made it clear the top job was mine if I could hold it."

There are aspects of New York he doesn't like, however. "We're paying $450-a-month rent for a house in New Rochelle during the season," he moans. "We paid $155 a month in Cleveland." During the off season, the Costello family still lives in Magnolia, Ohio, Vince's hometown, where he learned the game of football by playing on his high school's six-man football team.

Like many commuters, Costello works a five-day week, generally working nine to five from Tuesday through Friday and then putting in a grueling two-hour stint on the field on Sunday. The team stays together in a hotel on nights before the games; the players go to bed early, get up for a breakfast of steak and eggs and then go to the stadium a couple of hours before game time.

Though the players scrimmage hard and drive themselves to exhaustion before the season starts, once it gets under way their life—except on Sundays—is remarkably nonviolent. During the week, the 40 players, along with Coach Allie Sherman and his eight assistants, spend much of their time watching game movies to criticize their own play and become familiar with the play of their next opponent. They also spend a lot of time working out strategy. They do run through plays on the field, but they usually try to avoid hard contact.

There's good reason for the lack of combat. By the time the season starts, the players are in good shape and they know the plays well. A rough practice could result in an injury that might end a career and weaken a team. Vince Costello has missed very few games because of injury, but he worries constantly about his condition, which does reflect years of absorbing poundings by other burly pros and by foes of his Ohio University college team.

Among other things, Vince has a nagging back ailment, caused by gridiron battering, and an arthritic big toe that is the result of being stepped on by cleated giants. He has broken or dislocated four fingers. (Despite his ailments, Vince attacks the notion that pro football is a "dirty" game, with players out to injure one another. "The other guy has to make a living, too," he says. "Besides, the only thing you'll get trying to punch a guy wearing all that armor is a bruised hand.")

Except when he's in uniform, Vince now wears a heavy, buckshot-filled belt for back support. During the off-season, when he has no regular job, he exercises regularly to strengthen his back, though he says that in recent years he has been cutting down on his overall off-season conditioning. "That way, I'm not so beat come December," he says. But he usually stays in good shape all year round, never smoking and seldom drinking. He gains about eight pounds during the off-season.

There's nothing Vince can do to ease his toe pain, and he can't get his shoes off fast enough after a game. Dr. Anthony Pisani, the New York Giants' physician, says the toe may require corrective surgery after Vince quits football. As for now, says Vince, "it's just something I have to live with."

Another thing he has to live with is a bunch of big, ambitious young men who want to be middle linebacker for the Giants. It's enough to make a linebacker worry, but Costello professes to be unconcerned. "Listen," he says, "somebody's going to beat me out of my job one of these days, no matter what. I can't waste time worrying about it."

Vince actually helps out those who are trying to do him in. At the Giants' training camp at Fairfield, he conducted an impromptu class for linebackers in warding off blocks. Taking it all in was Henry Davis, a strong, rangy rookie from Grambling College who was Vince's chief rival for the Giants' middle linebacking job. Vince didn't seem to mind. "Davis has great physical equipment—great tools," the old pro says, but he adds knowingly: "But he's still got a few things to learn."

Davis could learn from just sitting around listening to Costello. A middle linebacker's job is to stop running plays up the middle, assist in stopping wider running plays and aid in pass defense. Vince says the biggest part of his job is to anticipate the offense's plays, and he confides he does this by keeping an eye on the guards and on the backs who line up behind the quarterback. If the guards and backs stand up and retreat before blocking, he'll usually drop back expecting a pass. If they move straight ahead, he'll look for a straight-ahead running play. If they swing to one side, he'll follow them, anticipating a wide run.

He says you have to be alert constantly. Teams like to shift assignments for blocking the linebacker, so you have to be on your toes "or you might not get up for the rest of the afternoon," he says. "You've got to know when to look for the tackle instead of the center, or whether an end likes to block low or high. The whole decision takes a fraction of a second, and if you're not alert you'll be beaten before you know it." He also says a linebacker must vary his own movements so the foe "won't know where he'll be."

When Henry Davis or some other youngster does beat out Costello, Vince probably will try to stay in football as a coach. He says he already has turned down one pro coaching offer. He has some experience. He was coaching high school ball at Big Walnut, Ohio, when his former college coach suggested he try out with the Browns, who then signed him as a free agent.

Football has been his life for many years, and leaving the sport entirely probably would be very difficult. Linebacker Sam Huff, who retired in 1967 after 12 years in the NFL, says the adjustment is painful.

Huff, who became a sales manager at a textile firm, makes about a third of what he was making as a well-paid football hero, but he says it isn't the money that troubles him. "You don't really appreciate the ego part —being cheered, seeing your name in the papers all the time, being recognized on the street—until you leave," he says. Costello isn't nearly as famous as Huff was, so Vince might not have such a painful adjustment. But he undoubtedly would miss what Huff calls the "something special about being part of a team of guys who all speak the same language and who appreciate what you're doing."

If linebacker Costello decides to become Coach Costello, his football pay will drop sharply, at least for a few years. With that in mind, he has been lining up several sidelines in recent years. In 1964, he, two Cleveland teammates and two lawyers opened a boys camp south of Cleveland. Vince owns 60% of the camp and draws $300 a month out of it; he expects this salary to increase eventually.

In addition, he and his two brothers, who live in Canton, Ohio, own two single-family homes and two duplexes there, which they rent. Vince also is a member of an investment club and owns a "fair-sized" portfolio of stocks, which he says, tapping his head, he manages himself.

Dr. Pisani of the Giants says that Costello, at 36, is in "amazingly good" physical shape, despite his ailments, and that he has "the agility and reflexes of a man a half-dozen years his junior." As such, Vince probably could make it with a pro team for a few more years, even though he already is past the age that most players call it quits.

Indeed, it probably will be family pressure or pressure from his outside interests that eventually will make Costello retire. He has six children. Costello has to spend two months away from his family each summer while he trains, and he says that this "gets harder as the kids get bigger."

His wife, Sally, says "the family is getting too large to haul back and forth between Ohio and New York every year." She has "said a few little things here and there" about getting Vince to retire, but "I guess he's not ready to hear them yet."

Mrs. Costello, a tall brunette, is interested in her

husband's job but confesses she doesn't really know what it's all about. "Some wives really talk the language," she says with some amazement, making it clear that she doesn't. She rarely misses a game that Vince plays in, but she says she doesn't really worry about his getting injured. "His mother worries about that enough for both of us," she says.

—FREDERICK C. KLEIN

Ships of Wood— Men of Iron

JOHN Paul Jones wouldn't recognize a nuclear-powered Polaris submarine if he fell over one. But the chances are he would feel at home in another "modern" vessel of the U.S. Navy.

It is built almost entirely of wood, and one man is always assigned to keep the hull's brass bolts snugly tightened lest the whole vessel fall apart. Wallowing along at a poky eight knots, it may take up to 42 days to cross the Pacific. Invariably, the deck leaks in a rainstorm.

The crewmen are a gamy lot—largely because they sometimes can't shower for a week at a time; the ship's fresh-water capacity is limited. So is its fuel supply. On long trips, it must rely on "the blob," a 2,500-gallon rubber bladder filled with reserve fuel and lashed to the deck. "You just can't make it without your blob," explains a crewman.

You often can't make it without seasick remedies, either. The vessel draws only 10.5 feet of water and in heavy weather tends to pitch and roll so hard that crewmen have to be lashed in place at their duty stations. Observes a former skipper: "Even if the ship's tied to the pier, and a duck swims by, the roll will almost knock you off your feet." He's not exaggerating much. At a change-of-command ceremony on one ship, several wives invited aboard got so ill they had to leave. The vessel was docked at the time.

This nautical nightmare is the ocean-going minesweeper, which is designed to seek out and destroy enemy mines before they can damage U.S. ships. Though the minesweeper sounds like a relic of earlier days, all 63 ships of this class have been built since the end of the Korean War, making these capricious vessels considerably more "modern" than many steel warships still on duty. A reminder of this brings only hollow laughter from many crewmen; they say the motto of the U.S. Mine Force ("Ships of Wood—Men of Iron") is an apt one, asserting that you need to be more than flesh and blood to serve on a minesweeper.

Many of the vessel's maddening problems are traceable to the new magnetic mines introduced by the enemy in the Korean War. Sensitive to the natural magnetic fields of steel-hulled ships, they blew up two metal minesweepers in the Korean conflict and induced the navy to build its "new" models with wooden hulls and as little ferrous—or iron-containing—metal aboard as possible.

The result is a partial throwback to the Bon Homme Richard command by John Paul Jones. In fact, some wags maintain that only sails and scurvy are lacking—and there are times when exasperated crews wish they did have sails. The minesweepers' diesels are largely of aluminum and other nonferrous metals, which are more subject to wear and bending than steel. Consequently, minesweepers spend a lot of time towing each other around while cursing enginemen try to get the finicky diesels shipshape again.

That's not easy either; a minesweeper's specially made tools are nonferrous too. They cost three times as much as ordinary tools and wear out twice as fast, grouses one engineering officer.

When not on actual minesweeping missions, the crew can enjoy some of the amenities of normal Navy shipboard life—like shaving with electric razors, watching movies or TV and listening to radio and piped-in music in the comfort of air-conditioning. But shavers, TVs, radios and all the rest have to go when there are mines to be swept; there's too much magnetism and ferrous metal involved. Left in the audio-visual void, some desperately bored salts have been known to while away the off-duty hours with a hot game of pick-up-sticks.

Most typewriters and even paper clips can't be aboard during sweeping. "I always thought the Navy would collapse without paper clips," marvels one officer. Another quips that jettisoning the typewriters probably makes the ship a lot more combat-effective.

It's all but impossible, of course, to operate a ship without at least some iron or steel aboard, even if it's only in radio tubes or food cans. Since even these small objects create a magnetic field around a ship, minesweepers are equipped with electric coils designed to offset the natural magnetism and reduce it to a level that won't set off most mines. This process is known as "degaussing." All manner of things can disturb the process, driving a crew to distraction.

Capt. Lewis Denny, a staff officer for the Pacific Mine Force, based in Long Beach, once commanded a ship that flunked its degaussing system check for four days in a row. After almost turning the ship inside out, someone discovered that crewmen had used magnetic shingle nails to put up pinups. The nails went overboard, and the ship checked out. Another skipper had to get rid of his pocketknife because technicians felt it could foul up the magnetic field.

The ship's degaussing system is so finely adjusted that crew members have to be careful even with permissible items. For example, cooks using canned goods have to put the used cans back on the shelves exactly where they got them, or the coils that continually offset the magnetic field of ferrous items will over-compensate and alter the magnetic balance.

Crewmen admit to finding some small compensations in minesweeper duty. For one thing, pictures can be hung on the wooden walls (with nonmagnetic alloys nails, of course), giving minesweeper sailors an artistic edge on their colleagues in ships of steel.

But the disadvantages outweigh the niceties. A minesweeper is crowded—a crew of about 70 in a vessel 175 feet long and 35 feet abeam—and the crew's eating area serves also as lounge, library, briefing room, movie theater and emergency operating room. There are only five or six officers on a minesweeper, and if they had to spend much time on all of the various duties technically assigned to them, they would be candidates for nervous breakdowns.

Consider the tasks assigned to Lt. (j.g.) Daniel Threlkel of the USS Pivot, which operates out of Long Beach. His primary job is ship's engineering officer—but he also is assistant damage control officer, maintenance and data collection officer, preventive maintenance officer, gas-free spaces officer, bulk drug custodian, audit officer and Protestant lay leader.

The leaky decks of the minesweeper (caulking is a lost art in most Navy shipyards) subject crewmen and equipment below decks to a steady drizzle when it rains, when the deck is scrubbed or when a wave breaks over the deck. "If the leak is over the executive officer's cabin, you've really got problems," laments one boatswain's mate.

Though the minesweeper is a seeming anachronism, Mine Force brass say it is full of ultrasophisticated electronics and other gear that make it more than a match for mines. Ideally, the ship passes right over the magnetic types and detonates them far astern with an electronic device trailing at the end of a long cable. Other types of mines can be detonated or cut from moorings with various gear carried on board.

The Navy has yet to put its assertions to the acid test, however. Though some small craft not designed for ocean duty have been used to cut mine cables operated by Vietcong dug into shore bunkers in Vietnam, no ocean-going minesweeper now in service has ever swept a mine in combat; they have never had the chance. Ocean-going minesweepers have seen battle duty in Vietnam, but only as patrol boats charged with intercepting enemy coastal shipping.

Some crewmen seem happy that they have never had to sweep a real mine. These sailors say its not unusual to see practice mines emit smoke flares beneath their ships during drills—indicating that a real mine would have blown the vessel to kingdom come.

—BYRON E. CALAME

A. J. Foyt, Man in a Hurry

A. J. FOYT JR. is a burly Texan who drives fast cars for a living because he loves it and is very good at it. But he doesn't like to talk about death.

It is always with him, though. Screaming along at 170 miles an hour, A. J. and his racing colleagues are often only a hairbreadth from flaming disaster. A slight error in judgment can do it—or the snap of a single bolt.

Early in 1968 in Phoenix, while testing tires for Goodyear Tire & Rubber Co., A. J. slammed into a wall at 160 m.p.h. A year before, in a race in Milwaukee, his car crashed and burst into flames. And a year before that, in a race at Riverside, Calif., he hit another wall when his brakes failed at 150 m.p.h.

A. J. has stayed alive through 18 years of racing, despite broken bones and severe burns. When he returned to his $75,000 home in Houston after the fiery Milwaukee smash-up, A. J. says he was "all covered with bandages," and when his three children came to greet him, "they just completely broke down in tears."

A. J. could quit. He has already proved his racing prowess and driving skill. In 1967, for the fourth time, he was named National Championship Driver by the U.S. Auto Club, and his third victory in the 500-mile Indianapolis Classic that year was a feat that only three other men have matched. All told, he has brought home more than $1 million in prize money, although the bulk of his earnings come from product promotion and testing.

A. J.'s wife, Lucy, clearly wouldn't mind seeing her husband bail out of the driver's seat for good. "It's like being the wife of a soldier in Vietnam," she says. "You never know if he's going to come home again."

But year after year at Indianapolis Lucy has been in the stands—watching her husband try to outrun the world's fastest racers on a track where 30 drivers have been killed since the first Indianapolis 500 in 1911.

If A. J. is ever scared, his full, friendly face doesn't show it. Like most top racing drivers, he shrugs off the threat of death and injury. "Look at it this way," he says, "you could just as easily be killed in a plane crash."

That's debatable, but there is no doubt that racing is an exceedingly dangerous sport. Since 1956, at least 15 of America's top drivers have perished in mishaps of one kind or another at major tracks—and that doesn't include an unknown number of "dirt track" drivers who test their bravado in jalopies on unpaved ovals in small towns around the country. Nor does it include sports-car racing drivers.

Some observers say drivers like A. J. keep racing because they are overendowed with a "competitive urge," and that racing is their way of seeing how far they can press their luck. But most devoted racing fans view it as just another sport, like football or baseball, in which individuals with extraordinary skills can put their talents to work.

Still, racing buffs concede that omnipresent danger helps account for auto racing's success. "No one is looking for a bad crash, but it's always in the back of your mind and somehow that adds excitement," says one fan at the Indianapolis Speedway.

Auto racing is the nation's second largest spectator sport, after horse racing. In 1967 auto races attracted some 40 million paying customers, compared with 31 million fans in 1962. That's still a long way from the 67.8 million fans who attended horse races in 1967, but auto racing officials say that their crowds are growing each year—even though they don't offer pari-mutuel betting.

As the crowds increase, so do the financial rewards for drivers. The good ones, like A. J. frequently become millionaires. A. J. declines to talk much about money, but associates estimate he probably earns more than $400,000 in a good year, including some $250,000 from testing and promotion contracts with auto, oil and tire companies. A. J. also has a sizable income from his investments in securities and from two Goodyear service stores in Houston that he owns and leases back to Goodyear.

Like almost all the other race drivers now in the big time, A. J. started on the dirt tracks. His father, who owned a garage in Houston, helped A. J. buy a motorcycle to race when he was 17. A. J. did well, and a year later, he graduated to jalopies. Later came "modified specials" (something like hot rods), midget racers and souped-up stock cars. In 1958, A. J. qualified to race at Indianapolis, and in 1961, he won the 500 for the first time.

A. J.'s stubbornness is something of a legend around the race track, and it has caused him some difficulty in the past. George Bignotti, a well-known and highly respected mechanic, says he left A. J. in 1965 because "he thought he knew more than I did about cars." Since then, A. J.'s father has been his chief mechanic.

A few of A. J.'s competitors say he is often rather distant and aloof from the camaraderie that usually exists among drivers. "He can be as nice as pie or as mean as the devil," adds mechanic Bignotti. But no one doubts that A. J. is dedicated to his profession. Racing writer Ken Purdy calls A. J.'s involvement with cars and racing "an obsession." He says he has known A. J. "to pass up a $1,500 speaking engagement just to run in an insignificant race in which he could win at most $600." Says A. J.: "There's really nothing else I want to do or ever wanted to do but race."

Despite his reserved manner, A. J., like many other drivers, has a legion of fans, some of them willing to work for nothing just to be near the action. A visitor to A. J.'s headquarters in Houston found John Fisher, an electrical engineer from San Francisco, and a Delta Air Lines pilot named Mike Ryan, from Memphis, working on his cars. Both men pay their own way to follow him around the racing circuit. "It's a special arrangement," says Mr. Fisher. "I work for A. J., and he lets me."

Many racing fans consider the life of a driver glamorous, but as Lucy Foyt suggests, it is nerve-racking for drivers' families. A. J. concedes that his mother constantly pleads with him to give up driving. And Lucy tells about the effects on their 12-year-old son, Tony. "Three weeks before Indy, he becomes very quiet and moody. He doesn't talk about it," she says. Even A. J. admits: "In some ways, racing comes before my family."

A. J. is usually gone from home seven months of the year, attending races or testing products. Even when he's in Houston, says Mrs. Foyt, he often leaves home at 7 a.m. and doesn't return until midnight—seven days a week. Still, Mrs. Foyt avoids trying to pressure A. J. into quitting. "He would probably drive us crazy—he's such a restless person," she says.

—DAVID BRAND

Daring Diver

IT'S half past midnight. Professional scuba diver August J. Faulstich Jr. is 70 feet underwater near Littleton, N.H., struggling to pry a one-ton steel grate from the bottom of a huge hydroelectric dam.

There are at least five ways that Gus Faulstich can die in the inky waters this night—and drowning might well be the least painful of them.

When freed from the dam, the steel grate will be lifted to the surface for cleaning, but a miscue by the crane operator above could mean crushing Gus between the grate and the dam face.

Gus is working at night, when electric demand is low and part of the hydroelectric project isn't operating. But if an engineer should disregard the red warning tags on his control panel and open certain underwater gates, the diver and tons of water surrounding him would be quickly sucked down a 200-foot-long tunnel to the turbine that turns a giant generator. The effect would be much the same as walking into a spinning aircraft propeller.

And there's also the chance Gus could fall victim to one of the professional diver's two greatest hazards—the bends (an imbalance of nitrogen in body tissues) or air embolism (in which air bubbles are forced into his bloodstream). Both can result from variations in water pressure on the diver's body. In the bends, a diver may face excruciating pain in his joints and muscles, paralysis and death within hours. An air embolism can lead rapidly to heart stoppage and death.

Gus knows these risks well, but in spite of them—maybe even because of them—he wouldn't trade jobs with any desk-bound land-lubber. "Not everything I do is exciting," he says. "But most of it is," he adds with a grin.

A well-muscled, blond-haired six-footer, Gus Faulstich (pronounced FALL-stick) is typical of a small breed of adventuresome young Americans who risk their lives at a wide array of underwater jobs to earn their livelihoods.

There are 8,000 to 10,000 professional divers in the nation, up some 15% to 20% from two years ago, says John Cronin, general manager of U.S. Divers Co., the world's biggest maker of diving equipment. (U.S. Divers is a California-based subsidiary of a French company headed by oceanographer Jacques Cousteau.)

Like other top professional divers, Gus possesses a wide range of blue-collar and white-collar skills. He can read blueprints, weld, do light construction work, do stress analysis and take motion pictures and still photographs—all underwater.

Born the son of a St. Louis florist, the 29-year-old diver never saw salt water until 1962, the year he ditched the bookish routine of a college freshman's life to come East and join the Coast Guard. He began scuba (for self contained underwater breathing apparatus) diving for pleasure and for some occasional pocket money while he was assigned to the Coast Guard Air Rescue Station at Salem, Mass. He loved diving so much that he signed on as a diver with New England Divers Inc. of Beverly, Mass., the very day, (Mar. 13, 1967) he was discharged from the Coast Guard.

In the four years since then, Gus has rapidly risen

to head up his company's four-man East Coast commercial diving division. His work experience has been widely varied—from teaching a socialite how to scuba dive to recovering bodies of drowning victims. He has inspected top-secret underwater defense equipment and even repaired an underwater power cable for nearly 24 hours straight with the air temperature at 10 below zero. (The power cable project was an emergency job to restore power to a coastal Massachusetts town. Without electric power, many furnaces in the town couldn't function.)

Gus shrugs off the potential hazards of his work—especially when he's talking about them in the presence of his pretty, honey-blonde wife, Maureen. He dwells instead on his love of the undersea environment as the main payoff in diving. "It's another world down there, man," he says. "No phones, nobody bugging you—just the quiet and the sensation of floating. No matter how tense I get on the surface, it all melts away when I go down there. I can pull myself together there."

Yet, as with other divers, he has found the thrill of risk a lure throughout his adult life. "When he was back in college, he and his roommate were talking about running off to become mercenary soldiers," says Maureen. "He didn't know whose side they wanted to fight on, but the adventure of a soldier's life attracted him."

While in the Coast Guard, Gus souped up his car to make it "the fastest machine on (Boston's) north shore," he recalls.

Though marriage and the birth of his daughter, Jennifer, seems to have settled him a bit, the urge for risk-taking even for fun emerges from time to time.

For example, on a Saturday morning not long ago Gus joined a group of four other divers at the New England Aquarium in Boston to test out some new diving equipment developed by U.S. Divers. Perhaps only to a group of professional divers would a 24-foot-deep aquarium tank containing a large and dangerous sea turtle, a nine-foot shark and a six-foot barracuda seem like an ideal place to test the equipment.

About 75 bug-eyed visitors—including Maureen and the baby—peered through the glass walls of the tank while divers worked in two-man teams, one testing the equipment while the other protected him from the aquatic creatures in the tank.

Gus casually avoided a near head-on collision with the shark, then spent the next 10 minutes grappling with the 150-pound sea turtle to keep it from attacking the other diver. As Gus maneuvered the tortoise toward the side of the tank, one woman spectator turned to a companion and said: "My God, how can anyone be crazy enough to do that?"

While the risks of his profession may be a lure to Gus, he's far from reckless in his approach to them. On the New Hampshire dam job—undertaken to remove the protective grates from the dam's water intakes so they can be cleaned and repaired—his caution is obvious. He laboriously goes through a step-by-step inspection of his own diving equipment and takes his three diver helpers through an equally thorough examination of theirs. He then checks with the engineers below to be certain they know what part of the dam the divers will be working on and, finally, discusses safety precautions with the crane operator. In all, the checks take more than 40 minutes before he is ready to don his diving gear.

Gus and his diving companion, Edgar Callahan, prepare to make the first of two dives scheduled for the night. During the first dive, the other two divers will stay at the surface to help direct the crane operator by relaying instructions received on a radio-like communications unit. Then the two diving teams will switch roles.

Each team will stay down a maximum of 50 minutes this night, since a longer stay at the 70-foot depth would invite an attack of the dreaded bends unless the divers are prepared to halt their ascent part way up and wait for up to a half hour for the nitrogen in their tissues to be dissipated. The divers aren't carrying enough air for such a wait.

Simply suiting up for the dive is a project in itself. Gus and Ed Callahan struggle to wriggle into protective "wet suits" made of ⅜-inch-thick foam rubber. First there is a pair of rubber shorts, then a body vest with hood, then a long-legged coverall type garment, then a zippered rubber jacket, another hood, two pair of rubber stocking-like boots, rubber gloves, swim fins, a web belt strung with 16 pounds of lead weights, twin metal tanks weighing 72 pounds, face masks and, for Gus, another special mask containing the microphone and earphones for the communications system. In all, the suiting-up takes some 15 minutes.

Thus laden with well over 90 pounds of equipment each, the two divers disappear into chilly dark water (temperature 54 degrees) and descend quickly to the 70-foot depth. Tenders on the dam above then lower a pneumatic power wrench to be used in loosening giant bolts that hold the grate in place. Gus's voice—punctuated by the measured, hissing sound of his breathing—calls for the crane operator to lower the cable.

In less than a minute, Gus and Ed have secured the inch-thick steel cable to the grate, and the whine of the power wrench mingles with grunts of exertion emitting from the speaker atop the dam. "This is beautiful tonight; I can't believe it! All the nuts are out," Gus shouts after a few minutes. "Take up the slack on the cable and try to lift it off the hooks," he says.

But when the instructions are relayed to the crane operator and he responds, the cable tightens dangerously without moving the grate. A corroded hook on the grate is wedged firmly into the wall of the dam.

After 20 frantic minutes of prying at the grate with a crowbar lowered from above, Gus's mood changes. "Jesus Christ—what a pain this is," he roars into the microphone.

After seemingly endless minutes, Gus successfully pries away the damaged hook, and the crane operator prepares to lift it to the surface. Just then, Gus's voice pipes up from the speaker. "Ed is out of air. I want you to lift him up on the cable with the grate. Do you understand?" The divers at the surface quickly reply and motion the crane operator to bring the grate to the surface and then stop. Seconds later, Ed Callahan surfaces and pulls himself from the water, his face white with exhaustion.

The underwater work environment is a difficult one at best. Bogged down by his equipment, a diver must be strong enough to maneuver effectively in the water.

In addition to the physical strains, in recent years divers have often found themselves with sharply limited underwater visibility due to water pollution. Both pollution from particulate matter in the water and from wild growth of algae, nourished by sewage, are on the rise in New England coastal and inland waterways, Gus says.

"Just in the years I've been diving, I've seen underwater visibility go steadily down," he says.

Due to rising concern about water pollution in New England, as elsewhere around the country, Gus has found himself increasingly faced with the odious mission of inspecting sewer outlets in rivers and the ocean to check the effectiveness of sewer plant operations. On such jobs, visibility rarely exceeds three feet and the diver may risk infections from his contact with improperly treated human wastes.

While the hazards of professional diving are evident, there are no reliable national statistics on diver deaths over the years. In fact, John J. McAniff, the diving officer at the University of Rhode Island's Department of Ocean Engineering, just in 1970 began the nation's first comprehensive study of diving deaths nationwide.

"No one really knows how often diving deaths have been classified by police and medical authorities simply as 'death by drowning' over the years," Mr. McAniff says. "We have evidence of 124 Americans killed in diving accidents in 1970, but there may have been a few more," he says.

"Several" of the diving deaths recorded by Mr. McAniff in 1970 involved professional divers, "but our data isn't clear on this point in some cases," he says. Diving companies, fearing legal actions, often "don't choose to report deaths among pro divers to us," he says.

While there have not yet been any actuarial tables compiled on professional diving deaths, insurers assume the profession to be high in risk and price their coverage accordingly. At one major life insurance company, Gus's premium costs for a $20,000 ordinary life insurance policy would run $534.60 a year. If he were an accountant or stock clerk, Gus could buy the same coverage for $384.60 a year.

"Divers are classed in our highest-risk category," says a spokesman for John Hancock Mutual Life Insurance Co.

For most divers, including Gus, pay is modest in relation to the risks and difficulties of the work. Since his salary is "not much more than $10,000 a year," Gus has turned to side pursuits to raise extra money. In the past three years, he has purchased three rental houses in Beverly, Mass., on which he's carrying over $60,000 in mortgages. The income from the houses "is just about offsetting our costs, and if real estate values climb we're hoping to sell the houses in a few years for a big enough profit to buy an apartment house," says Maureen.

Of course, some divers—about 2,000 of them in the U.S.—are highly paid. These are the men who undertake dangerous maintenance and inspection work on offshore oil drilling rigs along the Gulf Coast and West Coast.

These oil rig divers—the elite of the profession—commonly work at depths of more than 300 feet and often use underwater habitats to stay submerged for up to 10 days. By contrast, Gus rarely dives more than an hour or two a day and rarely goes below 100 feet.

Oil-rig divers are paid by the day and earn premiums for greater depths and longer stays below the surface, so their earnings mount quickly during the six to eight months of the diving season each year. "It's common for me to make about $1,000 a week during the season," says Nick Zinkowski, a free-lance oil-rig diver based in New Orleans. The 42-year-old Mr. Zinkowski has been diving professionally since 1948 and migrated to the Gulf Coast from New England six years ago.

"Sure, I'd like to make the money the guys on the Gulf Coast make," says Gus, "but I'm smart enough to know I don't have enough experience to get in that bag."

Many divers live as hard as they work, says Mary Kell, who edits Undercurrents magazine, a New Orleans-based monthly publication for professional divers. "Quite a few I know are also sky divers. They like nice boats, expensive watches, good clothes and fast cars," she says.

While Gus's life style is considerably lower-keyed than his more affluent Gulf Coast counterparts, it is grander than that of many Americans. He and a partner bought a 32-foot luxury boat that sleeps six. Gus used the boat for weekend diving excursions to nearby shipwrecks and even to take his wife out for the evening. "When you're doing some waterfront night clubs, the only class way to arrive is by boat," he says.

Gus says he has felt genuine panic only once during his diving career. The incident occurred in 1966 during a dive he made to secure heavy chains to a boat mooring in Beverly harbor. "I was in about 30 feet of water and my air started to run out. But I was so close to finished I thought I could just make it, so I continued to work for about another minute or so. Finally, I just had to have air so I shot up toward the surface," he recalls.

But 10 feet from the surface his tanks became snarled in several ropes that were fastened to the heavy chain on the bottom, "God, it was awful. I could look up and see the surface, but I couldn't reach it. Finally I came to my senses and unfastened my tanks and just left them there," he says. "I went straight home and got into bed; just left the diving gear right there where it was."

The next morning, Gus dove back down, got his gear and finished the mooring job. "I just had to go in right away. You can't let fear beat you like that," he says.

—TIM METZ